MATLASKE

Volume

Duncan Wood

All profits from the sale of this book go to

St Peter's Church, Matlaske

Copyright

Dedication

This book is dedicated to Donny March of Matlaske,

whose bravery is an example to us all

Contents

Introduction

This is a book for dipping into. Each chapter is self-contained.

There is a brief history of Matlaske from pre-historic days through to the Middle Ages, paying careful attention to Domesday.

If you're interested in military history, there's plenty of material on the men of Matlaske who fought and died in the Great War, on operations conducted from the RAF base here in the Second World War and on how one Matlaske man surprisingly found himself under fire at Omaha Beach.

If you prefer things ecclesiastical, there are brief histories of Matlaske and Barningham Winter churches and short biographies of some of their long-deceased rectors. We look in more detail at the 19th century Rectors of Matlaske and at one Rector who suffered great losses in both the First and Second World Wars.

There is a chapter about the now demolished Matlaske Hall, where members of my wife's family once lived for a few years.

My historical investigations were at first only about the village of Matlaske, but the links with Barningham Winter are so strong that of course I had to include that parish too. The modern civil parish of Matlask includes ancient Matlaske, Barningham Town and Barningham Norwood, so any future volumes of local history that I might produce will cover all three. Volume 2 is in fact already in preparation!

I am grateful to so many people who have helped me with information, advice or technical support. These include Derek and Freda England, Vera Norman, Jeremy Norman, David Longe, Jim and Marion Shepherd, Donny and Ruth March, Janine Harrington, Michael Argent, Thelma Wells, Jackie Bonfield, Mandy Wood, Ben Wood, David Wooff, and Tom Nightingale.

I'm also grateful to those organisations that have given permission to use or reproduce documents in their possession, such as the National Archives, the Norfolk Record Office, the Norfolk Heritage Centre and the National Library of Scotland. My thanks are also due to the myriad volunteers of Wikipedia (of whom I am one), whose writings I have borrowed in part and built upon in several places, and to military history enthusiasts who share information and insights on various excellent websites. Credits are given in the final chapter of the book.

Any mistakes in this book are of course entirely down to me!

I would encourage my fellow citizens of Matlask the civil parish to come forward with any memories or investigations that they would like to share; there are various ways of enjoying local history together, but if there are enough stories, we can produce more volumes like this one.

Duncan Wood, Matlaske

October 2020

Chapter 1

Origins of the village of Matlaske

Where better to start than with the Domesday Book, King William the Conqueror's great survey of England carried out in the year 1086?

Norfolk is included in the second volume of the survey, known as 'Little Domesday' because it contains information on only Essex, Norfolk and Suffolk. The world 'Little' is a misnomer, because it is in fact physically bulkier than Great Domesday, and is richer with information. In all probability, Little Domesday is the raw material that should have been digested into the much sleeker text of the Great Book, but never was – so much the better for posterity!

Matlaske is mentioned four times in Little Domesday.

The **first** mention is in a long series of entries about South Erpingham Hundred (a local government area defined in Saxon times, before the Conquest). The principal landowner is King William, who is also the local lord. The text says that in Matlaske (spelled here as Matelasc), Harold held 30 acres of land, worth 5 shillings. This refers back to ownership in the time of King Edward, before the Norman Conquest. Harold was a Saxon earl.

The **second** mention is in another group of notes on South Erpingham. This is a much longer note. King William is again principal landowner and local lord, the village name is spelled Matelasc. The text says that Matlaske is a berewick, a term denoting an outlying or specialised estate; the word is from the Old English and literally means 'barley wick'. The village has 1½ 'carucates' of land. A carucate is a measure of ploughland used for taxation, and is roughly the area of land that could be ploughed by a team of 8 oxen (in a day, presumably). The village, the Book says, has always had 7 villans, ie, villagers, peasants a cut above the rest, who are similar to free men but are not quite free because they are subject to the manorial court. There is 1 plough on the demesne (ie, the land belonging to the lord, who is the King), and 1 plough belonging to the men. There is enough woodland for 20 pigs. There are 15 sokemen in the village. These are freemen but who owe service to the lord of the soke, in this case, presumably, the King again. These sokemen hold 1½ carucates of land, 2 acres of meadow and woodland for 20 pigs. Confusingly, the Book now says that there have always been 4 ploughs. I assume that these are in addition to those owned by the lord and the villans. In the time of King Edward, the village was worth £4, later £6, but now in 1086 is worth £10 "blanched", ie, for tax purposes, and 20 shillings in exactions. The village is 1 league in length and 1 league in breadth and pays 12 pence in geld (ie, land tax). Confusingly, the next sentence says that Matlaske is 3 furlongs in length and 2 in breadth, and pays 3 pence in geld. As one league in medieval England equalled twelve furlongs, this only makes sense if we assume that Little Domesday is talking about two different parts of the village, one perhaps the lord's and the other belonging to some freemen.

The **third** mention is, oddly enough, under North Erpingham Hundred. Here the village is called Matingeles. Is this really Matlaske? Various scholars evidently think so, for that is how they translate it, and I think they are right for reasons that I shall explain shortly. The principal landowner for this piece of land is Count Alan Rufus of Brittany (about 1040-1093), who after the Conquest became the Earl of Richmond and built Richmond Castle in North Yorkshire. He was a second cousin of William the Conqueror twice over. The Little Domesday entry says that in Matlaske in the time of King Edward, a free man of Earl Harold's, called Estan, held 16 acres of land. There have always been 2 bordars there, the note says, with 2 oxen. (A bordar is a peasant rather lower in the economic pecking order than a villan.) Since the Conquest, the land is held by a man called Ribald, who, historians say, was Count Alan's brother. It is assessed (for taxation purposes, presumably) in Saxthorpe. Why this should be the case is not clear.

Alan Rufus, Earl of Richmond, swearing fealty to William the Conqueror in a 14th century illumination. Count Alan was a prominent landowner in East Anglia and one of the most powerful men in Norman England. He built the original manor house of Costessey Hall near Norwich, and is buried in Bury St Edmunds Abbey.

The **fourth** and final mention of Matlaske is in the same section of Little Domesday, and is rather dramatic. I think it must refer to the same estate as in the third mention, as they are of the same acreage, which is why I think 'Matingeles' is indeed a variant of 'Matlaske'. The Book says that in Matlaske (here spelled Matelesc), where Count Alan owns an estate, one man of the King's makes claim to 16 acres of land by offering judicial ordeal or battle against the Hundred, which testifies that the estate belongs to the Count. One of the Count's men is willing to prove that the Hundred is telling the truth, again either by judicial ordeal or battle. The word 'battle' sounds bad enough, but trial by ordeal was probably worse! There were two main forms of judicial ordeal. One involved being dropped into a deep pit filled with holy water. If you were innocent, you sank; if you were guilty, you floated. The other type of ordeal required you to walk a number of paces determined by the court, holding a red-hot iron in your hand. The burns were then bound up for a set time. When the dressings were removed, well-healed wounds pronounced you innocent, but septic ones declared you guilty.

Before the Normans

The Domesday Book gives us a picture of Matlaske as it was towards the end of the eleventh century. However, the village is older than that. The parish church has traits indicating a Saxon origin, and the name of the village itself comes from an Old English expression meaning 'The ash tree where meetings are held.' This suggests a focal point at which local people could meet to discuss matters of communal interest.

The archaeological evidence pushes us back even further. The earliest finds by field walkers and metal detectorists in Matlaske are a palaeolithic flint hand axe dating from 700 000 BC to 10 001 BC, and worked flints dating from the early Neolithic to the early

Bronze Age, ie, from 4000 BC to perhaps 2000 BC. These relics may, of course, come from itinerant populations, and do not necessarily show that a settlement or village was here.

However, there is a cropmark to the south of the village, near Hall Farm, which is thought to be a Bronze Age ring ditch dated between 2350 BC and 701 BC. A ring ditch is usually a round barrow that has been ploughed out over time; and if this barrow was a burial site, then in all likelihood a settlement was not too far away. There are also pottery sherds from the Iron Age (800 BC to AD 42) and Roman period (AD 43 to AD 409), which are stronger evidence of habitation. A gold coin from the late Iron Age has been found in the village.

The evidence for a settlement in the Roman period seems to me to be quite strong. In addition to the pottery sherds mentioned above, Jeremy Norman unearthed a Roman coin in his garden in the village in 1975. Since then, metal detectorists have also found a large number of Roman artefacts, including a dozen coins, a male figurine, a brooch, and an important example of a Roman metalsmith's claw-hammer.

Some artefacts have been discovered from the Middle and Late Saxon periods. In 1992, field walkers near St Mary's Church, Barningham Winter, found sherds of Ipswich and Thetford ware pottery. In 2001, detectorists in Matlaske came across a late Saxon strap-end with relief moulded decoration, dating probably from the centuries just before the Norman conquest.

Medieval Matlaske

The modern civil parish of Matlask is much larger than the old ecclesiastical parish, and includes Barningham Winter (also known as Great Barningham, Barningham Magna, or Town Barningham), a civil parish which was separate until 1935, and Barningham

Norwood, a civil parish which in 1935 was merged with Gresham but later transferred to Matlask.

The *village* of Matlaske is now smaller and less populated than it used to be even in the nineteenth century, and is essentially a string of properties alongside the southern edge of the Barningham Hall estate. In the Middle Ages it was much larger. Old maps and archaeological investigation suggest that the ancient and medieval village was to the north of the current Rectory. A hollow way, heading from north east to south west, might well be all that is left of the medieval village street. This street may have moved naturally to its current position as older buildings decayed, or might have been diverted for some reason. There is also a series of medieval and post-medieval earthwork enclosures, with banked, terraced and ditched boundaries, and some evidence of platforms on which buildings probably stood. All of these structures are judged to be medieval, but a late Saxon pot has also been found in the same area.

Post-Renaissance Matlaske

This is a topic that needs further research in the archives. For now, we should merely note that there are some historically interesting buildings still standing in the village, ranging from the 16th century to the 18th century in date. It would be good to understand these in their social and economic context.

Matlaske Hall, which was demolished around 1955, is considered in Chapter 10.

Chapter 2

Barningham Winter & Barningham Hall

Barningham Hall and its park are geographically central to the modern Matlask parish. There was a medieval great house which belonged to the Winter family, and which was demolished in 1612 when the present Hall was built. The medieval structure stood on the site of the lawn that now exists between the current Hall and the lake. When this site was still a field, ploughing revealed old brick and flint foundations; and more recently, the creation of a ha-ha between the gardens and the lawn has exposed an old wall. Aerial photography shows cropmarks in the area.

The land on which this great hall stood had come into the possession of the Wynter family by 1361, having previously been owned since the Norman Conquest by people named Curzun. We shall consider the Wynter family in a moment, but first we must look into the story of their predecessors.

At the time of the Domesday Survey, the parishes of Barningham North or Norwood and Barningham Winter were one. I have examined the Domesday entries for Barningham (and, for good measure, Little Barningham too) but I can find no mention of the Curzun name there.

Francis Blomefield, writing in the first half of the eighteenth century, is clear that the principal landowner in what is now Barningham Winter, immediately following the Conquest, was Roger Bigot (or Bigod), a Norman knight. Bigod took part in a successful campaign against Danish forces near Ipswich in 1069. He was appointed sheriff of Norfolk and Suffolk in 1074 after the deposition of the rebellious Earl of Norfolk, many of whose lands he acquired. The earldom seems to have remained vacant, but Bigod's son Hugh was appointed to it several years after Roger's death in 1107 and the earls seem to have remained the principal landowners for some time.

Blomefield also says that soon after the Conquest, the Curzun family was granted the local lordship in Barningham. There was a William de Curzun in the time of King Henry I, a Ralph Curzun in the time of Henry II, and a Sir Richard Curzun in 1239 under Edward I. Blomefield noted that it was in that same year that the name 'Tone Barningham' was first used, 'Tone' meaning 'Town'; Roger Curzi held three parts of an estate there of Richard de la Rokele, which he in turn held from the Earl of Norfolk. Was this Roger another member of the same family? Certainly, others named Curzun, John and Thomas de Curzun, had an interest there under Edward I. Roger le Curzun was lord of Barningham Town under King Edward II, who in 1296 granted a fair and weekly market for the township, and the right of free warren for blame-free hunting of game. In 1338, Robert de Burneby, the priest of Town Barningham, who seems to have been appointed as a trustee for the estate (which probably indicates that the last member of the direct Curzun line had died), settled the lordship on Sir John de Curzoun and his wife Elizabeth. The estate at this time consisted of a 'messuage' (a house and its outbuildings), 56 acres of land, 3 of meadow, 8 of pasture, 16 of heath, and 2 of alder. There was 13 shillings of rental income. The heir was a man called Roger, but around the year 1360, the estate was held by a John de Reppes, whose claim appears to have depended on the fact that he had married a 'Curzoun' widow.

I wonder whether the Barningham Curzuns were a branch of the Curzon family that settled in Derbyshire and eventually produced that rather grand statesman, George Curzon (1859-1925), 1st Marquess Curzon of Kedleston and Viceroy of India? Genealogical websites seem to think that this a possibility.

After John de Reppes, the Wynter family arrives on the terrain. William and Maude Wynter were the first of the new owners. William (about 1336-1398) served twice as sheriff of Norfolk & Suffolk. His son John (about 1364-1414) extended the family's holdings from the parishes around Town Barningham by the happy expedient of marrying four times, each of his brides bringing new estates with them - some lying beyond the borders of the county.

A lawyer by training, John Wynter became a valued administrator in the King's service, for example, as steward of the Duchy of Cornwall. From about 1400, he was adviser and treasurer to the Prince of Wales, Henry of Monmouth, who as King Henry V some years later would be the famous victor of Agincourt. During this period, John was elected to Parliament five times. His brother Robert seems to have stayed at home as Rector of Barningham. After the accession of Prince Hal as King, John Wynter was returned to Parliament twice more. In addition to his national duties, John helped many Norfolk friends with legal advice. He died in the winter of 1414 and was buried in Barningham church.

John's son, Edmund Wynter (who died in 1448), was also a lawyer. He was not as prominent on the national scene as his father had been, but was several times a Member of Parliament. One of the most interesting things about him, looking back with the plays of William Shakespeare in mind, is that he sold his father's manor of Loundhall in Saxthorpe to Sir John Fastolf, Knight of the Garter, who is thought to have been the inspiration for the Bard of Avon's great comic character, Falstaff.

Edmund Wynter seems to have served as a legal advisor to the second and third Dukes of Norfolk in the Mowbray line. Sometime in the 1430s, he married the wealthy widow of John Wodehouse (who, incidentally, was in all likelihood a distant ancestor of the humorous novelist and short-story writer, P G Wodehouse, the creator of Jeeves & Bertie Wooster, whose family originated from Norfolk). In 1443, Edmund joined the Duke of Norfolk and others in entering Norwich to suppress a riot, which sounds to have been rather more serious than the usual raucous Saturday night. He died in February 1448 and was buried in front of the high altar in Barningham church. The estate went to his son, another John Wynter.

The Wynter descendants eventually sold the Barningham house and lands to Edward Paston Esq (1550-1630), a member of the family of prominent Norfolk landowners which had its origins in the coastal village of Paston (where, incidentally, the author was married), and who left a treasure trove of fifteenth century letters for historians to pore over.

Perhaps the old Wynter house in Barningham had become decrepit with age, for Edward Paston promptly demolished it and in 1612 built the mansion that, with some later remodelling, stands today.

Edward Paston (I have found no good evidence that he was ever a knight) is an interesting figure. This generation of Pastons seems to have been particularly distinguished, for his first cousin, Sir William Paston (1528-1610) left a big mark on posterity as the founder of the Paston Grammar School in North Walsham (where Admiral Lord Nelson, another man with a Matlaske connection, was later educated). He was also a generous benefactor to Caius College, Cambridge.

Edward, whose godfather was King Edward VI, the commissioner of the Protestant Prayer Book for the Church of England, is noted for two things. One is his scholarly interest in music, and the other is his attachment to the Catholic Faith.

Edward Paston (1550-1630)

Paston was one of the earliest and most notable collectors of music in England. He stored these mainly at his Appleton house, near Sandringham, but also at his other homes, in Thorpe and Town Barningham. His taste was very conservative. He seems to have had a particular interest in pre-Reformation and mid-sixteenth century English composers, but very little in anyone later than Thomas Tallis - who died in 1585. The one great exception to this is the work of William Byrd, who died in 1623. Sir Edward owned several of Byrd's unpublished pieces and may well have known the composer personally. Indeed, some scholars think Edward wrote poems that Byrd set to music, including *Crowned with Flowers and Lilies*, a lament for the passing of the Catholic Queen Mary.

Edward's father, Sir Thomas, had been a Gentleman of King Henry VIII's Privy Chamber, and was probably the 'Mr Paston' – rather than Edward himself - who is recorded as teaching virginal playing to the Princess Mary. As Queen Mary, this former pupil of a Paston would, of course, restore the Catholic Faith temporarily.

Edward Paston was himself a distinguished lutenist, who could read not only the usual French style of music writing but also the Italian and Spanish systems. He seems not to have attended one of the ancient English universities, but as a young man to have travelled widely in France, Spain and Italy.

Edward had six sons and three daughters by his second wife, Margaret Berney. Three of these offspring entered religious houses on the Continent. His oldest son, Thomas, married Mary Browne, a member of a Sussex family which adhered to the old religion. Indeed, scholars suspect that it was Edward Paston who wrote a poem in memory of Mary Browne's devout Catholic grandmother, Lady Magdalen Montague, which William Byrd then set to music. A Paston grandson, also called Edward, was President of Douai College, a Catholic seminary, between 1688 and 1714.

In addition to owning Barningham Hall, Edward Paston owned the manor of Appleton and several other properties that had been left to him by his uncle, the distinguished sea-captain Sir Clement Paston of Oxnead. In the middle of the woods at Appleton, Edward kept a house where the Catholic Mass was celebrated. His niece, Mary Berney, a nun at Louvain, recounts how the Protestant English authorities came in search of recusants:

> 'It happened one day that the pursuivants came on a sudden and were kept in talk at the door sometime, whilst that the priest and the church stuff were put up safe into the secret place, so that coming in they found nothing. But they brought with them a bloodhound which stood snuffing about the secret place where the priest was. Before the searchers espied him comes a great cat and fell a fighting with the dog, never leaving

him till he departed from thence, which seemed an admirable thing that the poor cat was not afeared to set upon the dog. So would our Lord deliver them by this means.'

Edward Paston had local friends around Barningham, though he seems to have spent more time at Appleton and at Thorpe Hall near Norwich. His music collection was dispersed after his death. In 1669, a collection of songs and madrigals from Paston's library belonged to Stephen Aldhouse of Matlaske, who was one of the witnesses to Edward's will. Aldhouse also owned a second set of part-books that appear to be hastily made copies of originals in Paston's library. Many of Edward's musical manuscripts appeared for sale in the middle of the eighteenth century, presumably from various family members who were running short of funds.

Edward Paston died at the age of eighty and on 24th March 1630 was buried in Blofield church. His monument there reads:

> To Edward Paston Esq Second Son of S[r] Thomas Paston Knight one of the Gentlemen of Henry the eight his privy chamber truly noble noe lesse by stocke then all manner of vertue, most skillfull of liberall Sciences especially musicke and Poetry as also strange languages, Margaret his most loving wife and daughter of Henry Berney of Redham Esq alwaies mindfull of her most deare husband wth whom she lived most sweetly 40 yeares now alas in her funerall deprived of so great a solace of her life hath lamenting caused this howsoever a Monument of love to be set up.

Barningham Hall passed down the generations of Pastons until in 1736 Edward's great-great-grandson, another Edward (1693-1745), short of money for its upkeep, abandoned it. Eleven years after this Edward's death, the Hall and estate were sold to help pay off his debts. They were bought by William Russell, a whale bone merchant from London who made his money from ground bone fertilizer. In 1775 he sold the estate to one Thomas Lane, who himself ten years later sold it to Thomas Vertue Mott, to whose descendants it still belongs.

The great poet John Dryden, who rests in Westminster Abbey, wrote an Epitaph on Mrs Margaret Paston, of Barningham, Norfolk. This Margaret was, I think, the first wife of Edward Paston (1660-1713), the great grandson of the builder of Barningham Hall. She died at the age of 23, and was buried at Blofield. The epitaph is on her tombstone there.

Dryden's brief poem is interesting because its composition reminds us of how important Roman Catholicism remained in this branch of the Paston family even four generations after the building of Barningham Hall. Dryden himself was a convert to the Roman Church, and Margaret Paston, whose maiden name was Eyre, came from a prominent Catholic family. Indeed, two of her sisters became Carmelite nuns in Belgium.

Here is the epitaph:

So fair, so young, so innocent, so sweet,
So ripe a judgment, and so rare a wit,
Require at least an age in one to meet.
In her they met; but long they could not stay,
'Twas gold too fine to fix without allay.
Heaven's image was in her so well exprest,
Her very sight upbraided all the rest;
Too justly ravished from an age like this,
Now she is gone, the world is of a piece.

Barningham Hall and Rectory

The physical structure of the present Barningham Hall is familiar to Matlaske residents. It is the large mansion that was built in 1612 for Edward Paston. The west façade has a three-storey porch tower and, so Pevsner tells us, unusual two-storey dormer windows. The house was remodelled between 1805 and 1807 by Humphry Repton and his son, John Adey Repton. Humphrey's grave, incidentally, is prominent in the churchyard of St Michael's, Aylsham, beside the chancel door; his son is buried at Holy Trinity Church, Springfield, Chelmsford, Essex.

Barningham Hall is surrounded by a landscape park designed in the early 19th century by Repton. The park has an ornamental lake, belts of trees and an avenue. The formal gardens were close to the house, and Repton designed a raised terrace to the south of the house which, apparently, is the earliest 19th century example of this type of terrace in Norfolk.

The coach house and stables date to the 17th century with 19th century alterations. Repton also designed the early 19th century walled kitchen gardens, which have arched entrance gates.

Barningham Old Rectory is dated to about 1830. It looks to me like a smaller imitation of the Hall, with an attached stable block and coach house. Where did the Rectors of Barningham Winter live before this house was erected?

Chapter 3

Matlaske parish church and priests

Matlaske parish church, which is dedicated to St Peter, dates originally from the late Saxon period, after 850 AD. The building was augmented in the Middle Ages and restored in 1878.

The round tower is typical of the late Saxon and early Norman period, and in all likelihood the tower and nave were built together in the decades just before the Norman conquest. The tall and slender tower arch inside the church, built of brick and shingle, indicates a late Saxon date, as do the large flints and puddingstones in the corner of the nave between the porch and the tower.

Perhaps the most striking things about the exterior of the church are first, that it lacks a chancel, and second, that its tower, which is round, culminates in a curious octagonal belfry.

The absence of the chancel, the smaller part of a church at the east end which houses the sanctuary and altar, is easily explained. It fell down during divine service on 19th March 1726. That must have been a frightening experience. The walls fell outwards, which prevented any major injury to the congregation, though one wonders where the roof came to land. Some of the fallen stones were used to block off the east end of the nave, and some were added to the churchyard wall.

The church tower, with its oddly shaped top, reminds me of nothing so much as an Allen key. Architecturally, the style of the belfry is Decorated, which dates it to roughly to the first half of the 1300s. Perhaps the Saxon tower was refurbished at that time. The one bell that still remains was definitely in place in 1552, and probably dates from 1480, judging from its markings. It seems to be the work of Richard Brasyer the Younger of the Norwich bell foundry, who passed away in 1513. Sadly, the foundry closed after his death, and was replaced with a brewery; the residents of Norwich may have taken some consolation from it. There used to be three bells at Matlaske, but in 1741 the parishioners wisely removed two for safety reasons, especially as one was cracked. The remaining bell was refurbished as recently as 2005.

Internally, the church is also Decorated, so there may have been a major makeover in that period. The walls are of coursed flint dressed with stone. Externally, the style of the walls and the older windows is Perpendicular, which may indicate a slightly later date for the outer renovations.

In the walls of the church are rows of embedded tiles, narrow sides showing. One historian has suggested that these could be Roman tiles. However, this technique of strengthening mortar is used by modern builders when they wish to knit different patches of masonry together. It can be seen in much more recent buildings, including the author's home. It is likely that medieval builders used the same technique, and county archaeologists now deprecate the idea that the tiles in the church walls are Roman.

The church door is medieval, as are the baptismal font, the piscina (in which communion vessels would have been washed), and two of the windows.

The main roof dates from 1878. It is held up by eight corbels of stone-carved heads expressing various human activities or states of mind, ranging from the sacred to the profane: preaching; anguish (possibly at the length of the sermon); indulgence; peacefulness; devotion; being talkative; disappointment; and my favourite, being drunk.

The roof of the slightly detached-feeling south aisle is older, dating from 1710 according to a wall inscription. At the eastern end of this aisle is the splendidly plain Jacobean communion table that was retrieved from the ruined chancel in 1726.

The altar rails came from North Barningham when that church fell into disuse. A striking feature of the east end at Matlaske is the large brass chandelier which hangs just in front of the sanctuary.

Arms of King George III

Hanging above the south doorway (which now leads into the vestry, rather than outside) is a painted achievement (sometimes wrongly called a coat of arms) of King George III. What was the occasion for this? I was tempted to suggest that monarch's golden jubilee, which began in October 1809 and was widely celebrated, but the second quarter of arms shows the three fleurs-de-lys of France, the claim to which was formally dropped in 1802 after the Treaty of Amiens. I suspect, therefore, that the achievement dates from King George's accession to the throne in 1760.

Presumably, the vestry, on the south side, is the one built in the improvements and repairs of 1849-50, which also included a new window in the 'chancel', presumably meaning the sanctuary. These repairs cost Mrs Gunton, of Matlaske Hall, £300, at least £37,000 in modern money and probably rather more.

Notable burials in the church include many members of the Gunton family, who were the original occupants of Matlaske Hall. Another is of Richard Whitaker, the High Sheriff of Norfolk in 1725, who was interred in the church on 2nd December 1730.

I think it was probably this same Richard Whitaker who (posthumously) gave £200 in 1731 to augment the income of the Rector of Matlaske. That sum is probably equivalent to about £500,000 today, in terms of wealth. Queen Anne's Bounty (a fund set up by that Queen to help support the poorer clergy) also contributed £200, and the combined sum was used to buy just over 38 acres of land at Gresham, and just over 1 acre at Sprowston, according to White's 1854 Directory.

Old directories from the 19th century also say that Matlaske was a 'discharged rectory', a term indicating that the rector was exempt from ecclesiastical taxation. They also say that the Matlaske rectory was valued in the 'King's Book' at £5. This presumably is a reference to the *Valor Ecclesiasticus*, a survey of the revenue value of church property carried out on King Henry VIII's orders in 1535. Any rectory with an annual income of ten marks or more (roughly, £7) had to pay ten per cent of its income to the Crown (or, before the Reformation, the Papal Curia).

The Matlaske rectory also had some glebe land to support the Rector. In 1883, it was said to be 10 acres, but in 1854 it was only 8 acres. The rectory was also supported by tithes, a 10% tax on local agricultural produce. In 1841, following the passage of the Tithe Commutation Act, cash payments were substituted for the giving of agricultural produce, and the tithes were commuted for a revenue of £130 per annum.

The living of Matlaske was in the gift of the Sovereign, as Duke of Lancaster, and still is.

At the west end of the nave hang two funeral hatchments. These boards would have been on display outside the home of deceased gentry for six months or so before being moved to the church for permanent exhibition. There is contradictory evidence about whom these commemorate. The old church history leaflet by Mr Butler-Stoney suggests a man of the Gunton family who died in 1749, his wife following in 1804. I cannot myself find a married couple that satisfies those dates. Another observer (on Pinterest) has said that the hatchment bearing the words 'Resurgam' (Latin for 'I shall rise') is for Dennis Whitaker Gunton (1804-1848). This seems much more likely, as Mr Gunton's wife, Frances Mary Gunton née Thomlinson (1804-1869), meets the requirements of both outliving him and (according to Mr Butler-Stoney) coming from Cley-next-the-Sea. The other hatchment has a wholly black background, showing that both parties are dead.

Hatchment for Dennis Whitaker Gunton (1804-1848)

Many generations of Matlaske villagers lie in the churchyard. These include members of the Gunton family; various members of the Leeder family, who between them ran both the blacksmith's shop and the village grocery store and were 'overseers of the poor'; and an ardent Methodist preacher, James Bumfrey (1811-1865), a carpenter, whose gravestone says that he was 'a burning and a shining light' - a statement that came true, literally and spookily, when a bush surrounding his gravestone caught fire in a recent churchyard clearance.

Rectors of Matlaske

The carving on the Rectors Board includes a representation in wood of a niello that was found in a local field in the middle of the nineteenth century. Some sources say the find was made around 1847, others suggest 1852. A niello is an object made of precious metal decorated with black inlay. This one is golden, and shows a Crucified Christ between a bishop and St John the Baptist.

The board hanging in the church gives the following list of Rectors:

1305	Henry de Reding
1334	Richard de Carleton
1341	Nicholas de Hunworth
1355	John Attewell
13??	William Agell
1386	John Donne
1393	John Holbourn
1397	Robert Hoo
1427	John Lytelport
1458	John Tropewell
1474	Robert Brokenham

1483   Thomas Trylle

1525   William Kyngesmill

1544   Richard Smith

1574   John Brown

1601   Thomas Settle

????   Rowland Nicholson

1715   William Reynolds

1719   Thomas Gatlant

1741   Stanley Leathes

1793   Benjamin Suckling

1837   Arthur Langton

1872   Arthur James Richards

1883   Herbert Wynell-Mayow

1916   Joseph Whiteside

1942   Cyril Wilson

1949   Gwylim Albert Evans

1950   Carey Cooper

1956   Robert W S Close

1965   Ian Stratford Fairley

1975   William Paul Watkins

1976   Alan Clason Gates

1979   Stanley Frederick Hooper

1985   David Cecil Candler

1995   Paul Joseph Bell

2003   Michael Banks

2005   Philip Butcher

We know a little about some of these ancient Rectors.

Francis Blomefield, the 18th century historian of Norfolk, says that **Henry de Reding** (1305) and **Richard de Carleton** (1334) were presented by the Prior of Merton in Surrey. This Priory also had the patronage of Plumstead church, so the close connection of these two parishes is pretty ancient in origin. Merton Priory belonged to the Augustinian or Austin Friars, a religious order that worked in the wider community rather than in monastic seclusion.

Robert Bokenham (1474), **Thomas Trylle** (1483) and **William Kyngesmill** (1523) were all presented by the Bishop of Norwich. Each of these presentations is termed "a lapse", which suggests that the Priory of Merton no longer took care of the living but that the King had not yet taken control of it.

John Brown (1574) was presented by Queen Elizabeth I. It seems likely that his predecessor, **Richard Smith** (1544) was presented by Henry VIII in consequence of the English Reformation.

The Cambridge Alumni Books give us short biographies of some of the Rectors who were educated at that University, and also of Curates who served in the parish but whose names do not appear on the board in church. Here are brief details of some of these men:

Thomas Settle (1601) entered Queens' College at Michaelmas Term, 1575, as a pensioner, ie, with financial support. After graduating, he was ordained by Bishop Freake of Norwich. There is some evidence that he was Rector of Westfield, Norfolk, in 1579. He was also Minister at Boxted, Suffolk. His orthodoxy was questioned, and when he appeared before Archbishop Whitgift charged with preaching erroneous doctrines, he was actually imprisoned - from 1586 to 1592. On his release, he joined the Brownist congregation in London; as a result, he was again arrested and imprisoned in 1593. The Brownists were a kind of early congregationalist, and most of the dissenters who sailed to America on the *Mayflower* were of that persuasion. The Reverend Mr Settle obviously made his peace with episcopalian church order, however, for he became Rector of Barningham Winter from 1596 to 1614. He also became Rector of Matlask in 1601. He was probably the author of a work called *Tho. Settle, his Catechisme*.

Robert Tomson (1660) does not appear on the board in church – there seem to be some omissions, caused, perhaps, by the confusion of civil war, the abolition and restoration of the monarchy, and then the glorious revolution which ensured a Protestant succession to the throne. However, Cambridge University records show that the Revd Mr Tomson was appointed Rector of Matlask in 1660. He had entered Corpus Christ College at Easter, 1644, matriculating as a sizar, ie, a student who receives financial support in return for acting as a servant to other undergraduates. He originated from Norfolk, but we do not know where exactly. He graduated BA in 1648 and MA in 1651. He was ordained priest on 21st September 1649 by the Bishop of Kilmore, the Rt Revd Robert Maxwell DD, during the Commonwealth period. Mr Tomson was also Rector of Aldborough.

Thomas Bainbridge (1675) is another Rector missing from the board. He entered Christ's College as a sizar on 2nd April 1661, aged 18. He originated from County Durham, and his father was Cuthbert Bainbridge. He had been educated at Kirkby Lonsdale School. He graduated BA in 1665 and MA in 1670. He seems to have been ordained in the Diocese of London in May 1665, and then appointed Curate of Mepal in the Isle of Ely. He was (probably) Master of Holt School between 1667 and 1692. Appointed Rector of Plumstead and Matlask in 1675, he later he became Rector of Kelling St Mary and Salthouse St Nicholas. He died in 1714.

John Pearson (1675) – Curate, rather than Rector - was quite a local boy to this part of Norfolk, who entered Caius College, aged 16, as a sizar, on 14th September 1670. His (deceased) father was Richard Pearson. John had been born in Holt and educated there by Messrs Mazey and Bainbridge. He was able enough to be elected to a scholarship in 1674. He graduated BA in 1675 and was ordained deacon at Norwich in September of the same year. He then became Curate of Plumstead and Matlask. He later moved on to be (probably) Rector of Abbots Roothing, Essex, from 1682 to 1732 and also of Shelley from 1686 to 1732, the year in which he died.

Mordaunt Leathes (1769) was born in 1747. He was admitted to Corpus Christi College as a pensioner in June, 1764, from Norfolk. He matriculated in Michaelmas Term 1764; was elected to a scholarship in the same year; and graduated BA, 1764, and MA 1768. He was ordained deacon at Norwich in September, 1769; and priested, July, 1771. He became Curate of Matlask in 1769. He was then Curate of Erpingham in 1771. He was Rector of Itteringham from 1777 to 1807, and also of Mannington, 1779-1807; the two livings were consolidated in 1780. Mordaunt was the son of Stanley Leathes, who was Rector of Matlaske from 1741, and Alice Leathes née Cubitt.

Thomas Gallant (1719), shown on the board in church as Thomas Gatlant, I think, was admitted as a sizar (age 17) at Caius College in September, 1712. He was the son of Henry Gallant, a clothier, of Aldborough, Norfolk, where he was born. He went to school in Aylsham, where Mr Wrench was the master. Thomas matriculated at Caius in 1712; he was a scholar, from 1712 to 1718; graduated BA 1717, and MA in 1721. He was ordained deacon at Winchester in June, 1717; and then priested at Ely in March 1719. He was Rector of Matlask between 1719 and 1741; then of Blickling, 1732-61; and of Burgh-by-Aylsham, 1741-61. He died in November 1761 and was buried at Blickling. He had a brother called Robert.

John Lloyd (1780) was admitted as a sizar, aged 24 at St John's College in June 1780. He had been born at Llanwennog, Cardiganshire, and schooled in Carmarthen. No residence in Cambridge is recorded for him, and his name disappears off the records in February 1788. This suggests that he was a 'Ten-year man', that is, a mature student who could go straight to the Bachelor of Divinity degree after ten years, without first graduating BA and MA. He was ordained priest at Norwich on 6th August 1780, and became Curate of Plumstead and Matlask in the same year. He appears to have moved on to Dedham, Essex, where according to college records he died in 1813, 'aged 55' (the arithmetic is not quite right).

For more details of nineteenth century Rectors, see Chapter 6. For a brief life of the first Rector to arrive in the twentieth century, a man who suffered two great losses, see Chapter 7.

Chapter 4

Barningham Winter parish church and priests

The medieval church in the grounds of Barningham Hall is dedicated to St Mary. It is in a peaceful and pastoral place, but the Decorated period tower and roofless nave are dramatic-looking ruins. The south porch is also roofless, but elaborate, and its outer step is actually a medieval coffin slab. Under the tower arch, but still largely exposed to driving rain, stands an octagonal font. The church had already become quite ruinous by the early seventeenth century. The chancel, which is still in use, dates from the same period as the nave, but has a western extension which was probably erected as part of the 1874 restoration work. This extension houses an impressive gallery. The chancel still includes its original arch, plus a blocked ogee priest's door and sedilia and piscina under four moulded arches. There is an early 15th century brass to John Wynter, floor tombs from the 17th and 18th centuries and some early 19th century Gothic-style memorials. Members of the Paston, Mott and Radclyffe families are commemorated. Behind the altar, there is a war memorial reredos, and the east window has the arms of King Charles in stained glass. Opinions differ as to whether the Charles in question is I or II.

Rectors

1311   Simon de Beckham, instituted, presented by Roger le Curzon, of Tun-Berningham.

1324   Roger de Gunton. Ditto.

1329   Robert de Burneby, by Sir John Curzoun.

1347   Bartholomew Franks. Ditto.

1370   Roger Stephens, by William Wynter.

1407   Robert Winter, by Sir Thomas Erpingham, Sir Ralph Shelton, and Sir Robert Berney.

1412   Thomas Perer, by John Wynter.

1457   William Reed, by John Wynter, Esq.

1459   John Barley. Ditto.

1466   Robert Wale, by John Wynter, Esq.

1478   John Clement, by John Wynter, Esq.

1478   John Bekon. Ditto,

1485   Robert Sudcock. Ditto.

1490   Henry Ganton. Ditto.

1527   Thomas Tooke, by Henry Wynter, Gent.

1540   Robert Pyctow. Ditto.

1544   John Smith.

1552   John Philipson, by John Wynter.

1555   Jeffrey Turner, by the Bishop, a lapse.

1561   William Dawson, by Philip Wynter, Esq.

1570   Martin Bullock. Ditto.

1572   John Browe. Ditto.

1596   Thomas Settle, the Queen, by lapse. (see biography below)

1614   Samuel Thornton, A. M. by Thomas Settle.

1663   Richard Cleburn, A. M. by Henry Bedingfield, Esq. and Sir Henry Bedingfield, Knt. – see biography below

1680   James Clough, by Sir Henry Bedingfield, Knt.

1714   Thomas Plumsted, by Gresham Page, Esq. (see biography below)

1749   John Girdleston, by John Goodman, Gent.

1750   Matthew Lane, by Jos. Lane.

1759   Francis Copeman, by John Jermy

1760   Theophilus Buckridge, by Lord Anson

1764   Matthew Lane, by William Russell

1797   John Browne Wright, by the Bishop (lapse)

1807   Castres Mott Donne, by J C Mott

1819   John Anthony Partridge, by J C Mott

1830   William Robert Taylor, by J C Mott

1843   Edmund Nelson Rolfe, by J C Mott

1851   James Richard Anderson, by J C Mott

1866   James Wilson, by J C Mott

1875   Edward James Harper, by J C Mott

1884   John Riley Mee, by J C Mott

1910   William Shemin Cleather, by J C Mott

1933   Cyril Wilson, by C C Mott-Radcyffe

1949   Gwillym Evans, by CC Mott-Radclyffe

1950   Carey Cooper, by CC Mott-Radclyffe

1956   Robert Struther Close, by CC Mott-Radclyffe

1965   Iain Stratford Fairley, by Sir Charles Mott-Radclyffe

1975   William Paul Watkins, by Sir Charles Mott-Radclyffe

1976   Canon Alan Clason Gates, by Sir Charles Mott-Radclyffe

1979   Stanley Hooper, by Sir Charles Mott-Radclyffe

1985   David Cecil Candler, by Sir Charles Mott-Radclyffe

John Barley (1459) or Barly, was at Gonville Hall, Cambridge, which is now part of Gonville & Caius College. He graduated BA in 1461, MA in 1465, and Doctor of Divinity in 1476. He became a Fellow of Gonville Hall in 1466 and – very distinguished – was its Master from 1483 to 1504. He was Rector of Barningham Winter from 1459 to 1466, having been presented to the living by John Wynter. He was Rector of Winterton from 1479 to 1504. This overlapped with being Rector of St Michael Coslany, Norwich, from 1501 to 1504. He died in 1504 or 1505, and was buried at St Michael's. He was evidently a wealthy man, as he was a large benefactor to his college's buildings.

William Dawson (1561) matriculated as a sizar at Christ's College, Cambridge, in November 1554. He was Rector of Town Barningham from 1561 to 1570, and of Hackford (a share in the benefice of Reepham, Norfolk) from 1563 to 1583.

Thomas Settle (1596) entered Queens' College at Michaelmas Term, 1575, as a pensioner, ie, with financial support. After graduating, he was ordained by Bishop Freake of Norwich. There is some evidence that he was Rector of Westfield, Norfolk, in 1579. He was also Minister at Boxted, Suffolk. His orthodoxy was questioned, and when he appeared before Archbishop Whitgift charged with preaching erroneous doctrines, he was actually imprisoned from 1586-92. On his release, he joined the Brownist congregation in London; as a result, he was again arrested and imprisoned in 1593. The Brownists were a kind of early congregationalist, and most of the dissenters who sailed to America on the *Mayflower* were of that persuasion. The Reverend

Mr Settle obviously made his peace with episcopalian church order, however, for he became Rector of Barningham Winter from 1596 to 1614. He also became Rector of Matlask in 1601. He was probably the author of a work called *Tho. Settle, his Catechisme*.

Samuel Thornton (1614) matriculated as a sizar at Trinity College, Cambridge, around 1601, graduating BA in 1607 and MA in 1610. He was ordained deacon at Norwich on 22nd May 1608, aged 24, becoming Curate of Felsham. He was priested on 11th June 1609. He was the Rector of Wyville with Hungerton, Lincolnshire, from 1612 to 1632. In 1614 he also became Rector of Barningham Winter, a living he seems to have occupied until 1663. In 1632, he also became Vicar of Erisby, Lincolnshire.

Richard Cleburne (1663) was admitted to Jesus College, Cambridge, as a pensioner on 9th May 1631. He was from Huntingdon, had the same name as his father, and was baptised at Stanwick on 2nd June 1616. He matriculated in 1631, was elected to a scholarship in the same year, graduated BA in 1634 and MA in 1638. He was ordained deacon at Peterborough on 10th March 1638, and priested on 30th May 1640. He became Rector of Billingford, Norfolk, in 1642 and was Rector of Barningham Winter from 1663 to 1680.

James Clough (1680) was the son of a medical doctor, Gervase Clough, who originated from Ashton, Lancashire. James himself was born at Winwick, though whether this was the place of that name in Cheshire, Cambridgeshire or Northamptonshire is not clear; probably Cheshire. James was educated at Winwick School. He was admitted as a sizar at Caius College, Cambridge on 2nd July 1667, aged 21 and matriculated the same year. He was a scholar from 1668-71, graduating BA in 1671 and MA in 1674. He was ordained deacon at Norwich in July 1671, and priested on 24th December of the same year. He was Rector of Houghton, Norfolk, from 1671. From 1680 to 1713 he was Rector of Barningham

Winter. Between 1686 he was also Rector of Suffield. He died on 28th December 1713.

Thomas Plumsted (1714) was admitted as a Sizar at Caius College, on 21st May 1690. He was the son of William Plumsted (1646), a clergyman, of Wickmere, Norfolk, but had been born at Calthorpe. He was educated at a school in Wickmere run by Mr Robert Pate and at one in Holt run by Mr Bainbrigg. He matriculated at Caius in 1690, was elected to a scholarship between 1690 and 1695, graduating BA in 1694. He was ordained deacon at Norwich on 23rd September 1694, and priested on 7th June 1696. In that year, he also became Vicar of Briston. In 1714 he became Rector of Barningham Winter, a living he occupied until the year of his death, 1748. His will was proved in the same year.

Matthew Lane (1750) was admitted to Jesus College as a sizar on 4th November 1743. Originally from Suffolk, he was the son of a deceased clergyman. He matriculated in 1744, and was awarded a Rustat Scholarship as a clergy orphan; the famous poet Samuel Taylor Coleridge also held such a scholarship. He graduated BA in 1748, and was ordained deacon at Norwich in December of the following year. He was priested in December 1750. He was Rector of Barningham Town from 1750 to 1797, Vicar of Field Dalling in 1758, Rector of Welborne from 1763 to 1800, and Rector of Scoulton from 1764 to 1797.

John Browne Wright (1797) was born at Downham, Norfolk, the son of William Wright, a surgeon. He was admitted as a sizar, aged 17, at Caius College, Cambridge, on 28th July 1789; he became a pensioner the following year. He was educated at Brandon School (Mr Wright), King's Lynn (Mr Lloyd) and Newport, Essex (Mr Buck). He was elected to a scholarship in 1789 but did not matriculate until Michaelmas 1791. He graduated BA in 1794 and MA in 1797. He was ordained deacon in 1794 and priested at Norwich on 9th July 1797. He was Rector of Town Barningham from 1797 to 1807. He was also Curate of Rusper, Sussex, in 1801. He was the author of a book rather plainly entitled *Sermon*. He was the father of Walter M Wright, who also seems to have become a clergyman. John Wright died on 20th March 1846 in Brunswick Square, London.

Castres Mott Donne (1807) was admitted as a pensioner of Caius College aged 18 on 2nd July 1801. He was the son of Castres Donne, a clergyman, of Broome, Norfolk, where he had been born on 9th April 1783. I wonder whether there is a connection between this family and the John Donne who was Rector of Matlaske in 1386? (And were they all related to the famous metaphysical poet John Donne of the seventeenth century? *Batter my heart, three-person'd God*, and all that.) Young Castres went to school at Scarning in Breckland, under the tuition of a Mr Priest, appropriately enough. He matriculated at Michaelmas in 1801, was a scholar from 1801 to 1807, graduated BA in 1805 and MA five years later. He was ordained deacon at Norwich on 21st September 1806, and priested on 20th September of the following year. He married Frances Manning, the daughter of the Rector of St Peter's, Thetford. He was Vicar of Hempnall from 1807 and also Rector of Barningham Town from the same year. He was a good classical scholar who took pupils for college. He died on 11th June 1819, and was buried at Hempnall.

William Robert Taylor (1830) was from Earl Stonham, Suffolk, the son of the Revd William Taylor. He went to school in Norwich and was admitted to Jesus College, Cambridge, as a pensioner, aged 18, on 26th March 1821. He matriculated that year, and graduated BA in 1826. He was ordained deacon at Norwich on 18th June 1826, and priested on 10th June of the next year. On 24th June 1828, he married a Miss Beckwith of Holt. He was the Perpetual Curate of West Beckham 1829-43, and Rector of Town Barningham from 1832 to 1843. Alas, he died rather young on 23rd August 1843, at Holt.

Edmund Nelson Rolfe (1843) was the son of the Revd Robert Rolfe of Hempnall, Norfolk, where Edmund was born. He went to school in Norwich. He was admitted as a pensioner at Caius College, Cambridge, in 1829, aged 19. Matriculating that year, he graduated BA in 1833 and MA in 1841. He was ordained deacon at Lincoln on 22nd December 1833. He was Curate of Holme-Hale, Norfolk, from 1841 to 1842. He was the Rector of Town Barningham from 1843 to 1850, and then of Morningthorpe until 1884. He passed away on 25th April 1884, aged 73. He had a brother, Robert. The forenames 'Edmund Nelson' suggest a connection with the Nelson family, to me.

James Richard Anderson (1851) was born at Northaw, Hertfordshire, the son of Thomas Anderson, and went to school in Bury St Edmunds, Suffolk, under a Mr Donaldson. He was admitted as a pensioner at Trinity College, Cambridge, on 1st April 1842. He matriculated later that year and graduated BA in 1846. He was ordained deacon at Ely in 1846, and priested at Worcester (unusually far away) the following year. He was the Rector of Town Barningham from 1851 to 1866. He was also Perpetual Curate of West Beckham from 1856 to 1866. In 1866, he became Rector of Melton-cum-Felbrigg, a post he held until 1872, the year of his death. He is buried at Melton. He had a son, Arthur.

James Wilson (1866) was born at Inverness, the third son of a local banker. He went to school in Edinburgh and was admitted as a pensioner at Jesus College, Cambridge, aged 17, on 27th May 1854. He matriculated in Michaelmas Term of that year. Graduating BA in 1858 and MA in 1861, he was ordained deacon at Norwich in 1860 and priested the following year. He was Curate of Denton, Norfolk, from 1860 to 1863, and then Curate of Newton-in-the-Isle, Cambridgeshire, for the next three years. He was Rector of both Town Barningham and West Beckham from 1866 to 1875. He then became Vicar of St Stephen's, Norwich, until 1892. Following that, he was Rector of Barking with Darmsden, Suffolk, from 1892 to 1904, doubling that post with the Perpetual Curacy of Needham

Market until 1900. He died on 4th September 1904 at Inverness. He had a son, Thomas E Wilson.

John Riley Mee (1884) was born on 27th April 1848, the son of the Revd William Chapman, Vicar of Hayton in Nottinghamshire. (Why the different surname?) Mr Mee went to Uppingham School and was admitted as a pensioner at Christ's College, Cambridge, on 17th November 1866. He matriculated in Michaelmas Term 1867, graduating BA in 1872 and MA in 1875. He was ordained deacon at Rochester in 1873 and priested the following year. He served as Curate of Chrishall, Essex, from 1873 to 1878, then of Knipton, Leicestershire, from 1881 to 1884. He became Rector of Town Barningham in 1884, and of Barningham Northwood in 1891, serving both parishes until 1908. Towards the end of his life, he lived at Brandiston Hall, Alderford, Norfolk, where he died on 14th October 1921.

Chapter 5

Soldiers named on the Matlaske War Memorial

In this chapter, we have brief biographies of the seven Matlaske men who lost their lives in the Great War, which lasted from 1914 to 1918 (the Armistice, a ceasefire) or to 1919 (the Treaty of Versailles, which legally ended the War).

ALFRED WALTER GEE, Number 302607, H Battalion, the Tank Corps, died 30 March 1918 and buried at the Hedauville Communal Cemetery Extension, Grave H21

Alfred Walter Gee was born in 1887 and was baptised at Matlaske church on Sunday 13th March of the same year by the Revd Herbert Wynell-Mayow.

Walter's parents were John Gee (1844-1896) and Harriet Gee née Davison (1848- 1929). John was a labourer. Harriet had been born in Wickmere, and had worked as a housekeeper there before marrying John in the church of that parish in 1876.

John and Harriet had four children: Jane Sarah (1877-1964), Robert William (1881-1963), Alice Mary (1803-1946) and Alfred Walter, whom this article commemorates. He seems to have called himself Walter rather than Alfred.

In 1891, Walter was living with his mother, father and siblings Robert and Alice in Matlaske. A lodger, 39 years-old Thomas Steward, also lived with the family.

Sadly, Walter's father John passed away in March 1896 aged 51, and was buried in Matlaske churchyard.

By 1901, Walter, aged 14, was a stable boy. He lived on the Street, Matlaske, with his mother and brother Robert in the home of Thomas Steward, their former lodger, who was a teamster on a local farm. Harriet was by now Thomas's servant; but six years later, she would marry him.

At about the same time as his mother re-married, Walter too entered into wedlock - with Rhoda Amelia Bowman (1882-1944) on 18th February 1907 at Whinburgh, near Dereham. The marriage certificate shows Walter as a gardener, resident in Whinburgh. Rhoda was a spinster, born in July 1878 at Mattishall. Her father was a labourer.

The 1911 census shows the young couple living at Whinburgh, where Walter was a groom on a farm, training horses. They had one son, Robert, aged three.

Walter's handwriting

When war arrived in 1914, Walter felt the call of his country to military service.

Not many of Walter's Army records survive, but the Roll of Individuals entitled to the British War Medal and the Victory Medal indicates that he first of all joined the 26th Battalion of the Royal Fusiliers with number G/66310 and the rank of Private. Following the invention of the tank, he transferred to the H (that is, the 8th) Battalion of the Tank Corps with number 302607.

There is some evidence from *Soldiers Died in the Great War 1914-19* that Alfred Walter was at one time in the Royal Army Service Corps with the number 275385. However, I have not been able to find anything else to support this.

The Battle of Cambrai

Walter would certainly have taken part in the first ever armoured attack in military history, namely the Battle of Cambrai in 1917.

On 20th November 1917, the British Third Army launched a concentrated and tactically radical attack at Cambrai, where ground conditions were far more favourable than any seen to date. Following a surprise hurricane artillery bombardment, 378 Mark IV tanks smashed through the Hindenburg Line, temporarily creating the chance for a breakthrough. However, insufficient mobile reserves could get through in time to exploit the tanks' success, and within days the chance of changing the course of the war decisively had gone.

In fact, the Tank Corps had deployed its entire strength of 476 machines. They were led by the Tank Corps General Officer Commanding, Brigadier-General Hugh Elles, in a Mk IV tank called 'Hilda' – named after his favourite aunt, apparently.

The 8th Battalion War Diary tells the story of the actions in which Alfred Walter Gee almost certainly received the mortal wounds that took his precious life.

Walter and his comrades were trying to stop the Kaiserschlacht – the German Spring Offensive on the Western Front, which had been made possible by the collapse of Russia in the East, thus freeing up more German troops to fight the British, French and Americans in France and Belgium.

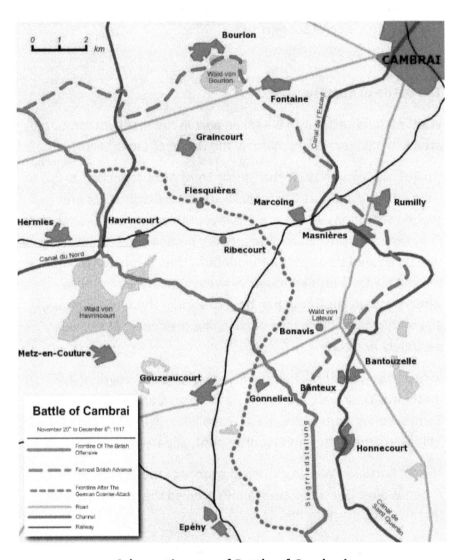

Schematic map of Battle of Cambrai

The Kaiserschlacht – The German Spring Offensive 1918

A Mark IV tank of H Battalion ('Hyacinth'), ditched in a German trench while supporting the 1st Leicestershires, during the Battle of Cambrai, 20 November 917

The H Battalion War Diary tells the amazing story in a fast-moving narrative: -

PARA 4 – GERMAN ATTACK, 21ST MARCH, 1918

As the middle of the month was passed, the nightly artillery fire increased in volume and it was generally felt that things were working up to a climax and that the bursting of the expected storm would not be long deferred. On the night of the 20th-21st an intense bombardment began before midnight increasing in volume as the hours went by and shortly before dawn shells began to fall along the line of the road by which stood the camp while a large number could be heard passing overhead towards the back areas. The Battalion stood to arms at 4-30 a.m. according to the custom which had prevailed for some time previous and by this time the noise of artillery fire from the direction of the line was so tremendous that there was little doubt that the attack had come at last, although news of any kind from the front was entirely lacking.

PARA 5 – SITUATION AT MID-DAY

About mid-day rumours came through to the Battalion that the enemy attack had swept completely through the main defence system and that DOIGNIES Village had fallen. As this place lay little more than 3,000 yards distant on the dominating ridge N.E. of the Camp the capture would render the position of the Battalion in VELU WOOD very doubtful and accordingly Major Pratt, DSO., MC., and Captain GUILLAUME were sent out to reconnoitre the situation. On their return they reported that the enemy were seen to be approaching in mass formation over the ridge beside the BAPAUME-CAMBRAI road N.W of BEAUMETZ but that DOIGNIES was said to be still held by our outposts.

PARA 6 – COUNTER ATTACK ON DOIGNIES, 21ST MARCH, 1918

Shortly after 1-0 o' clock, orders were received that 12 tanks would co-operate with the 19th Division in a counter-attack on DOIGNIES and two sections each of "A" and "B" Companies were warned to prepare for action under the command of Major E.D. BLACKBURN, MC. At 4-15 p.m. the Composite Company moved from VELU WOOD to its pre-arranged assembly position below the ridge S. of DOIGNIES Village with instructions to await further orders from the 57th Infantry Brigade. All the Tanks were in position in time to move off with the assembled Infantry at the ZERO Hour of 6-40 p.m. but night was already beginning to fall and it was obvious that their work would be both difficult and of doubtful value. However, in spite of the darkness and the dense mist which prevailed, making it impossible for the drivers or gunners to see more than a yard or two in front of them, all the Tanks got into action and inflicted serious losses on the enemy advancing on the East and South of the village. Apart from the casualties which it caused, the main value of the Tank attack was that it dis-organised and checked the rapid advance of the enemy and seriously deranged the pre-arranged time-table of his offensive in this area.

PARA 7 – BATTALION WITHDRAWN TO HAPLINCOURT

One Tank only failed to return to the rallying point, which was in a copse a few hundred yards west of VELU WOOD. Here the Composite Company joined the remainder of the Battalion which had also moved to this point. At 5-0 a.m. on the 22nd "A" and "B" Companies moved back to HAPLINCOURT some 3,000 yards S.W. of VELU WOOD, where the crews were accommodated in the huts belonging to the 2nd and 10th Battalions. The remaining Company under Major BENNEWITH was held in reserve to the 19th Division in the Copse near VELU WOOD ready to co-operate in a rear-guard action if necessary. During the evening the Infantry began to retire and "C" Company was ordered to rejoin the Battalion at HAPLINCOURT where it arrived at 2-0 a.m. the following morning.

PARA 8 – MOVE TO BANCOURT-REINCOURT LINE.

During the night orders were received for the Battalion to withdraw before dawn to the valley lying between BANCOURT and REINCOURT, south of the BAPAUME-HAPLINCOURT Road as the infantry were expected to retire to the high ground around DELSAUX FARM. By sunrise on the 23rd, the Tanks were in position and carefully camouflaged beneath the ridge while the crews got what rest and sleep they could in preparation for the incidents of an immediate future which was already destined to be stormy in the extreme.

PARA 9 – DEMONSTRATION BEFORE BUS, 24TH MARCH, 1918

The Battalion was now under the orders of the 2nd Infantry Division and early on the morning of the 24th instructions were received detailing two Companies to make a demonstration against the BUS-BARASTRE Line in order to allow of the withdrawal of the

Infantry from the now very dangerous BERTINCOURT Salient. At 9-0 a.m. "A" and "B" Companies moved off towards VILLERS AU FLOS while "C" Company was ordered to support the 6th Infantry Brigade in their consolidation of the RED LINE. The approach route of the first two Companies was under direct observation by the enemy and very heavy shell fire greeted their appearance on the ridge N.W. of VILLERS AU FLOS, while the German Infantry being warned of the impending attack, retired some distance and left their guns to deal with the Tanks. The attack upon Bus village had to be delivered over perfectly open country under very heavy direct fire from the hostile artillery and although the demonstration undoubtedly served its purpose and by checking the German advance enabled the infantry to extricate themselves from a most perilous position, the casualties to the Battalion were considerable and many Tanks received direct hits.

PARA 10 – OPERATION AGAINST HAPLINCOURT, 24th March, 1918

Meanwhile, "C" Company had gone into action in support of the 6th Infantry Brigade, two Sections operating between HAPLINCOURT WOOD and BARASTRE village and two directly against HAPLINCOURT Village and wood. Considerable casualties were caused to the enemy but owing to the retirement of the Infantry the Tanks were left without support and the survivors withdrew to their rallying point. In this section also the attack was made in the face of direct artillery fire and over 50% of the Tanks were hit.

PARA 11 – MOVE TO COURCELETTE

On the evening of the 24th all remaining Tanks of the Battalion rallied at GEUDECOURT west of the BAPAUME-PERONNE road but as it was discovered that the enemy had already occupied LES BOEUFS Village 2,000 yards to the S.E. it was deemed advisable to continue the withdrawal to COURCELETTE on the BAPAUME-ALBERT road. The route was now across the shell-torn wilderness of the old SOMME battle field and the going was slow and arduous.

Every road was choked with steady streams of Infantry, guns and transport all pouring towards the golden sunset sky and behind the retiring army the Eastern sky was full of the black reek of blazing and abandoned camps and Stores. At last, the long ribbon of the BAPAUME-ALBERT road was seen limmering *(sic)* white in the moonlight and by 2-0 a.m. on the 25th all the remaining Tanks and personnel had arrived at the rallying point. Major GROUNDS, DSO, established a defensive position with the tanks, none of which had sufficient petrol to proceed further while the remainder of the crews under Major PRATT D.S.O. M.C. set out to march to AVELUY village, N. of ALBERT, going on next day to ACHEUX.

PARA 12 – MOVE TO ACHEUX

Early on the morning of the 25th petrol and stores arrived just in time to enable the tanks at COURCELETTE to extricate themselves from the dangerous position in which the rapid encircling movement of the enemy was involving them, and this party also reached AVELUY in the afternoon. Here it was taken under the command of Major Bennewith and after a short rest, proceeded on the way to ACHEUX through fields and village where women and children gazed wide eyed at the passing tanks. A halt was made for the night among the fields W. of BOUZINCOURT and about 11 p.m. orders were received for all Officers and men, with the exception only of skeleton crews to man the tanks, to proceed at once by lorry to ACHEUX with every available Lewis Gun. Here the party rejoined the remainder of the battalion and was able to enjoy six hours much needed sleep in the village. At this time Lt. Col. Willoughby relinquished command of the battalion and was succeeded by Major D.H. Pratt, D.S.O., M.C. who took over on the night of the 25th at ACHEUX.

Alfred Walter's death of wounds is recorded in the Diary too:

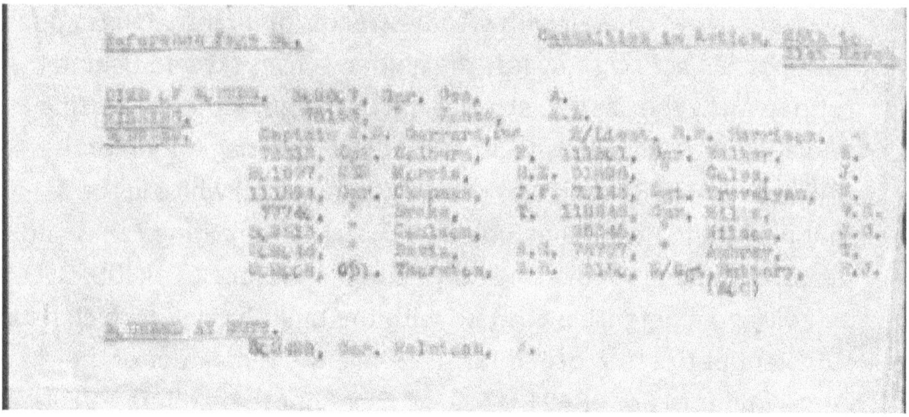

Walter, shown here in the top line with the rank of Gunner, might have been wounded at Courcelette on 25th March just before fresh supplies of petrol arrived allowing the British tanks to escape German encirclement. Alternatively, he might have been wounded earlier during the British counter-attacks on 24th March against German positions on the line between Bus and Barattre and at Haplincourt. British tanks were badly damaged by enemy shell fire during these actions.

I am inclined myself to think that Walter was fatally injured during the heavier fighting on 24th. His rank of Gunner indicates that he probably operated a Lewis machine gun. The 'female' Mark IV tanks had five of these. The 'male' Mark IV tanks had three machine guns and two 6-pounders.

Death and burial

Walter died of wounds on 30th March 1918.

The motto of the Tank Corps was "Through mud and blood to the green fields beyond", and Walter was buried amid the greenery of the Hedauville Communal Cemetery war graves extension, near the town of Albert – and close to the Somme battlefield of 1916.

Walter was mourned in England by his wife Rhoda, his children Robert Walter and Edith Maria, his mother Harriet and his sisters.

Harriet continued to live in Matlaske, and died in 1929.

HERBERT PARDEN, Number 14550, 9th Battalion, Norfolk Regiment, Died 18 October 1916, Buried at Bancourt British Cemetery, Pas de Calais, France – Grave VI.L.1

Herbert Albert Parden was born in 1896 in Buxton, Norfolk. His father was Albert Herbert Parden, a farm labourer, and his mother was Edith Mary Parden née Barnard. However, Herbert was not christened until 28th July 1901, when he was baptised - along with his brother William and sister Blanche - at Banningham parish church.

At the time of the 1901 census, Herbert, aged 4, was staying with his Barnard grandparents and their unmarried children at their home in Skeyton. His grandfather, James Barnard, aged 50, worked as a teamster on a farm.

By 1911, Herbert was living at Dog Corner, Little Barningham. He was a farm labourer like his father, and had two brothers, William (14) and James (6), as well as a sister, Blanche (9).

Herbert joined the 9th Battalion of the Norfolk Regiment. The 9th Norfolks were part of Kitchener's New Army, initially a part of the 24th Division but from October 1915 in the 6th Division.

Herbert must have joined up quite early in the war, given that he was entitled to the 1915 Star. He presumably landed at Boulogne on 30th August 1915 with the rest of his Battalion.

Herbert was killed in the same operation, the Battle of Le Transloy, the final phase of the 1916 Battle of the Somme, as another member of his battalion from Matlaske, Walter Ernest England (whose story we shall consider further down). The 6th Division were tasked with taking two German trenches, named MILD and CLOUDY by the British, but failed to do so. The section on Walter England, further on, gives the battalion commanding officer's explanation for this failure; here is the divisional general's assessment.

SECRET

XIV Corps.

I have gone very carefully into the causes of our failure to capture MILD and CLOUDY trenches between the 12th and 18th October.

1. The weather was bad, and aeroplane observation and air photos were impossible except on two fleeting occasions.
2. Unfortunately the air photos of these particular trenches were failures.
3. As a result, the German trenches were not accurately crumped, and we did not know what we were up against in the matter of trenches.
4. But over and above this difficulty of observation, there were other causes:-
(i)   The assembly trenches were poor and difficult to get out of owing to the wet, in spite of the steps which had been cut.
(ii)   The men were consequently late, and did not follow close enough under the barrage, and they were caught by the enemy's Machine Guns which were in his front trench.

(iii)   Nevertheless, our men got into the enemy's trench in each attack, i.e. on the 12th, 15th and 18th; but were, on each occasion, driven out by counter-attack.

5. That the assembly trenches were poor was due to the large number of practically untrained officers and men in the battalions.

    One whole night, for instance, was wasted in digging an assembly trench in the wrong place. The digging had also to be executed on a forward slope under constant artillery and Machine Gun fire, and sniping from both flanks as well as from the front.

6. The failure to get out of the trench in time and to follow close under the barrage, as well as the failure to hold the trench when captured, was also due to the inexperience of officers and men.

7. I am satisfied that if our battalions had been as well trained as they were when we came down to the SOMME, or if we had had longer time in which to train the new entry, we should have captured and held our objectives at the first attempt in spite of the difficulty of observation.

8. The officers who we receive to replace casualties are complete strangers to the rank and file who come out. I suppose it is not possible to train them together; but if it could be managed it would greatly facilitate and expedite the training of the new entry.

9. The Divisional and Brigade Schools had to be closed down when we went to the SOMME owing to the difficulty of finding accommodation for them – yet it is just at this very time, when the Division is suffering severe casualties, that these Schools should be working at the highest pressure.

C Ross

Major General, Commanding 6th Division

Photograph of the last page of General Ross's memorandum

Later, Herbert's body was found buried on the battlefield, near Gueudecourt. In the trench map on the next page, the spot is given by map reference N27.b.2.5. You are unlikely to be able to find the spot with just this reference, given the compressed copy of the map used here, so an alternative is to say that the place is in the top right-hand quadrant of square 27, where several lines cross just to the right of the letter 't' in **Gueudecourt**.

The Graves Registration Unit placed a wooden cross on the spot, bearing Herbert's name and number. The cross may also have had Herbert's tags attached to it. In 1919, the War Graves Commission used this cross to identify Herbert's remains and move them to his final resting place at the Bancourt British military cemetery.

(Previous page)

Excerpt from Trench Map showing the site of Herbert's original battlefield burial, at the intersection of several lines above the 7 in the number 27, and to the upper right of the t in 'Gueudecourt'

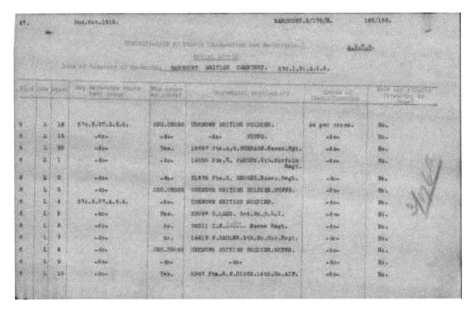

Record of exhumation and reburial of Herbert's remains

(fourth line down in the table)

JOHN GEORGE HANNANT, Number 41768, 10th Battalion, Durham Light Infantry, Died 9th April 1917, Buried at Tilloy British Cemetery, Tilloy-les-Mofflaines, Pas-de-Calais Grave III.J.5

John George Hannant was born in Matlaske on 5th December 1891. His father was James Hannant, a shepherd and cattleman, originally from Cawston; his mother was Emma Elizabeth née Grand, from Saxthorpe. The couple were married, probably in Wickmere church, in 1880 and had moved from that parish to Matlaske by 1885. John Hannant was christened in Matlaske church on 7th February 1892.

The family – there were three sons and two daughters in the 1901 census – lived in a house on the Street. By 1911, John was himself a farm labourer. However, he moved away from Matlaske and by 2nd October 1915, the date on which he joined the Army, he was living in Nottingham at 5 Garden Terrace, Denman Street. He was employed on his own account. Unfortunately, Army records do not say what his trade or business was.

John joined the Durham Light Infantry for the duration of the war, and was assigned to the 10th Battalion of that Regiment as number 41768.

John Hannant's signature on his Army recruitment form

The 10th Durham Light Infantry was a service battalion of Lord Kitchener's New Army, formed originally at Newcastle on 22nd August 1914. It was part of the 43rd Brigade and 14th (Light) Division. When John joined up, the Battalion had already been in

France for four months so he was presumably posted there in a draft of reinforcements.

Not much of John's service record survives, but we can trace the events of his last day alive from the 10th Battalion War Diary and trench maps.

John was killed during the first day of the Battle of Arras in 1917 – specifically, during that part of the first phase known as the First Battle of the Scarpe, which ran from 9th to 14th April 1917.

Wikipedia gives a good overview of the Battle of Arras:

"The Battle of Arras (also known as the Second Battle of Arras) was a British offensive on the Western Front during World War I. From 9th April to 16th May 1917, British troops attacked German defences near the French city of Arras on the Western Front. The British achieved the longest advance since trench warfare had begun, surpassing the record set by the French Sixth Army on 1st July 1916. The British advance slowed in the next few days and the German defence recovered. The battle became a costly stalemate for both sides and by the end of the battle, the British Third and First Army had suffered about 160,000 casualties and the German 6th Army about 125,000."

The map on the next page shows the overall geography of the Arras Offensive. John was killed in fighting for a German trench that ran down from Feuchy (centre of the map, just east of Arras) to Wancourt (centre of the bottom half of the map). The 10th Battalion Durham Light Infantry advanced eastwards roughly from Beaurains to a point south-east of Tilloy les Mofflaines. (John's body is now at rest in the British military cemetery of Tilloy.)

The Battalion War Diary, further below, spells out the details of the action in which John died. It might, however, be useful to give a summary here. The battalion had been sheltering in caves at Ronville, just north of the small town of Beaurains. On the 8th April they were ordered to go to the Assembly Trenches, specifically Bramble Trench, in readiness for going over the top. I have not been able to establish exactly where Bramble Trench was, but from the angle of the Battalion's subsequent advance it was most probably in the dark front-line trench due south of the word 'Ronville' in the trench map on page 68, below. The battalion's orders were to take first Nice Trench in the German lines, and then a network of reserve trenches known to the British as The Ark (all its individual trenches had been named after animals). This line of attack took the battalion past a trench formation known as Löwen Schanze, or Lion's Hill, where there was some enemy shelling, but most German resistance seems to have occurred at Nice Trench, where several British men were killed – among them, presumably, John Hannant.

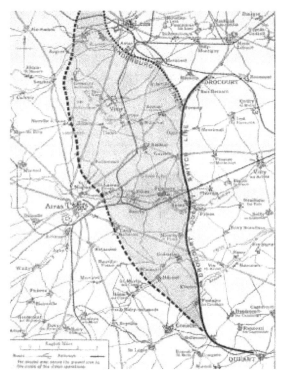

Map of the overall Arras Offensive

British machine gun position at Feuchy, just east of Arras

10th BATTALION D.L.I. WAR DIARY

Place	Date	Hour	Summary of Events and Information	Remarks and references to Appendices
In the Field	8-4-17 9-4-17		Battalion left RONVILLE Caves between 8.0 & 10-PM and moved forward into Assembly Trenches. 1./ The Battalion was settled in Assembly Trenches in F.E. Line & BRAMBLE Trench by 11.PM. With exception of a little shelling about LOWEN-SCHANZE on the way up we were not	

disturbed in any way by the enemy.

2./ 2nd Lts Braidford & Bill patrolled the enemy wire on our front between 12 midnight & 3.AM 9th April. Reports were forwarded to Bde H.Q.. Enemy seemed alert and cutting the wire by hand was not possible.

3./ At 9.34AM the Battalion advanced in 4 Waves – 1st wave followed by 2 Lines of Moppers Up (D.C.L.I.) all waves in Extended Order (5-paces) except the 4th which moved in Artillery Formation of Half Platoons

4./ The leading waves halted under the Barrage for some minutes and went into the first objective on top of it. The wire was practically obliterated in most places – in others it was an obstacle.

5./ The enemy put up some opposition on NICE Trench as we suffered from Rifle & Machine Gun fire 2 Captains – 2 Subalterns were wounded and 2 Coy

Sergt Majors were killed besides others.

6./ The Enemy put up practically no Barrage. What there was was on TELEGRAPH HILL on which some four Tanks were halted. Not a round was fired at the Tanks during their movement to ASSEMBLY in daylight as far as I saw.

7./ About 8 A.M. Battalion H.Q. moved to NICE TRENCH but as the advance was going well I left a Signal Station here under the Signalling Officer and followed after the Battalion with remainder of H.Q. to N.7.d.48.45

8./ The Battalion in advancing from NICE TRENCH bore to the left slightly and finished up at BLUE LINE at N.7.d.9.7 to N.7.d.9.1 in touch with K.S.L.I. on right. In the advance from Red Line to BLUE LINE was a big gap between us, and the Brigade on the right. & Telegraph Hill Trench south of Horse Lane and The Light Railway was never attacked.

			9./ The Battalion then reorganized. 2 Companies holding Blue Line in Front before mentioned (in para 8) and 2 Companies in Support from N.7.d.35.65 to N.7.a. 10./ During the advance to Blue Line there was a little hostile Barrage and not much sniping & Machine Gun Fire. The Enemy was Chiefly in his dug outs waiting to surrender.	
In the Field	9-4-17		*Continued.* 11./ Telegraph Hill Trench about Mule Lane South, not having been attacked was still occupied by The Enemy and a Machine Gun about N.13.2.99.90. 2 Vickers & Lewis Guns were therefore brought into action from N.7.2.5.5. and cleared this part of the Trench by Enfilade Fire. However, a Machine Gun and Odd Snipers continued to fire on us intermittently from positions beyond the Blue Line but their fire was mostly harmless.	1 Case – C E Stewart died 10-4-17

67

			12./ During the advance the Battalion captured & brought home 4 Machine Guns. Prisoners captured included men of 162nd, 163rd and 31st Regiments. 13./ Our estimated casualties for the 24 hours ending 10.P.M were 2 Captains & 3 Subalterns wounded plus & 142 O.R.	

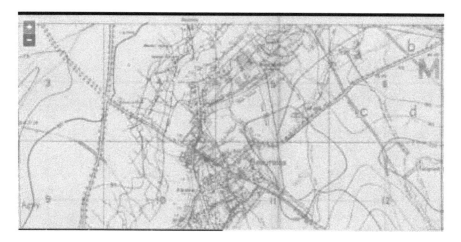

British Trench Map, March 1917. The top row of this map is row M. Squares within the row have a number, rising as you move to the right: the top row has 3, 4, 5, 6, the bottom row, 9, 10, 11, 12. Each square (eg M6) has four sub-squares, named a, b, c and d, always in that pattern.

The trench map is hard to read when not printed in colour. The British trenches on this map are on the left, the German on the right. The spaghetti-like mess shows just how complex the trench systems were. Ronville is at the top of cell M4b. Löwen Schanze is in square M5d. Nice Trench is just off the map to the right of square M6d.

The battalion's first objective was to take NICE Trench. Its second objective was to take the network of trenches known as The Ark. Enemy artillery fire fell on Telegraph Hill, nearby. John's body was originally buried on Telegraph Hill but was later exhumed and placed in Tilloy British Cemetery nearby.

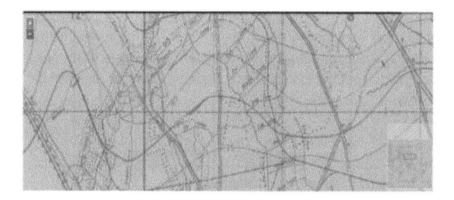

Nice Trench is about a third of the way across the top. The Ark trenches are about two-thirds of the way across the bottom of the map

Telegraph Hill and Nice Trench are in the centre of the map below, in squares M12b and N7a to N7c. Again, it is not very easy to read the map in black and white, but one can recognise the most important features. The most likely explanation for the facts we know is that John was killed trying to take Nice Trench, and was given a battlefield burial on Telegraph Hill.

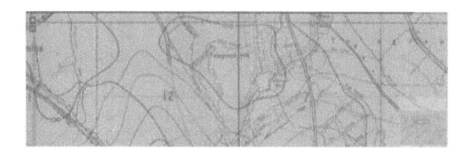

Map showing Telegraph Hill and Nice Trench

John is now buried at Tilloy British Cemetery, Tilloy-les-Mofflaines, in the Pas de Calais department of France. His grave is III.J.5, near the Great Cross. The inscription on his gravestone, chosen by his mother, is 'Safe in the arms of Jesus'.

John Hannant's grave

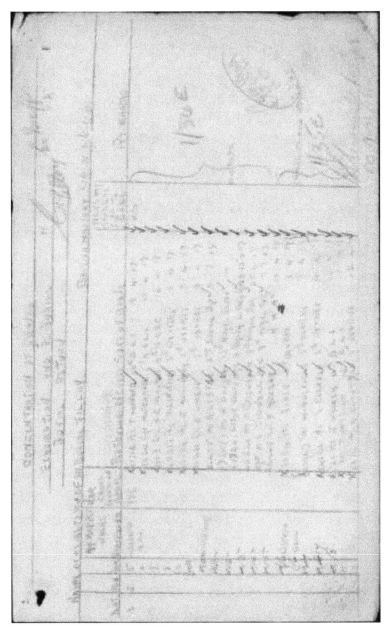

Record of John Hannant's battlefield grave (shown as T Hannant)

Private Stanley Claude Lee, 12th Norfolk Regiment, Service Number 320930, Died 24th December 1917, Buried at Jerusalem War Cemetery, grave C.21

Stanley Claude Lee was born at Itteringham in the summer of 1895 but he was not baptised until he was about five years old. The christening took place in the parish church there on 13th May 1900.

Stanley's parents were Robert Lee, a farm labourer, and Elizabeth Lee née Margetson. Stanley was the second of ten children. In 1901, they were living in The Bakers Rows in Itteringham, but by 1911 the family had moved to Matlaske, where Robert was now employed as a shepherd. Stanley, aged 16, was by this time a farm labourer.

Stanley was not unacquainted with death as a child, for his younger sister Olive died in 1900 and his sister Beatrice was born and died in 1906.

Not many of Stanley's Army records survive, but we know that he enlisted in Norwich and was ultimately assigned to the 12th Battalion of the Norfolk Regiment.

The 12th Battalion was part of the Territorial Force, so Stanley might briefly have been a part-time soldier before the War in its predecessor unit, the 1/1st Norfolk Yeomanry. This dismounted unit served overseas in the Egyptian Expeditionary Force's campaign in Palestine and on 11th February 1917 was re-formed there as the 12th Battalion (Norfolk Yeomanry).

The new Battalion was assigned to the 230th Brigade, 74th Division and XX Corps of the Egyptian Expeditionary Force.

It seems clear that in the 12th Battalion, Stanley would have fought in at least the Third Battle of Gaza and the Battle of Jerusalem.

Wikipedia offers a brief summary of the fighting at Gaza:

"The Third Battle of Gaza was fought on the night of 1st / 2nd November 1917 between British and Ottoman forces during the Sinai and Palestine Campaign of World War I, and came after the Egyptian Expeditionary Force (EEF) victory at the Battle of Beersheba had ended the Stalemate in Southern Palestine. The fighting occurred at the beginning of the Southern Palestine Offensive, and together with attacks on Hareira and Sheria on 6th – 7th November and the continuing Battle of Tel el Khuweilfe which had been launched by General Edmund Allenby on 1 November, it eventually broke the Gaza to Beersheba line defended by the Yildirim Army Group. Despite having held this line since March 1917, the Ottoman Army was forced to evacuate Gaza and Tel el Khuweilfe during the night of 6th / 7th November. Only Sheria held out for most of the 7th November before it too was captured."

And this is what Wikipedia has to say about the Battle of Jerusalem:

"The Battle of Jerusalem occurred during the British Empire's "Jerusalem Operations" against the Ottoman Empire, in World War I, when fighting for the city developed from 17th November, continuing after the surrender until 30th December 1917, to secure the final objective of the Southern Palestine Offensive during the Sinai and Palestine Campaign of World War I. Before Jerusalem could be secured, two battles were recognised by the British as being fought in the Judean Hills to the north and east of the Hebron–Junction Station line. These were the Battle of Nebi Samwill from 17th to 24th November and the Defence of Jerusalem from 26th to 30th December 1917. They also recognised within these Jerusalem Operations, the successful second attempt on 21st and 22nd December 1917 to advance across the Nahr el Auja, as the Battle of Jaffa, although Jaffa had been occupied as a consequence of the Battle of Mughar Ridge on 16th November.

This series of battles was successfully fought by the British Empire's XX Corps, XXI Corps, and the Desert Mounted Corps against strong opposition from the Yildirim Army Group's Seventh Army in the Judean Hills and the Eighth Army north of Jaffa on the Mediterranean coast. The loss of Jaffa and Jerusalem, together with the loss of 50 miles (80 km) of territory during the Egyptian Expeditionary Force (EEF) advance from Gaza, after the capture of Beersheba, Gaza, Hareira and Sheria, Tel el Khuweilfe and the Battle of Mughar Ridge, constituted a grave setback for the Ottoman Army and the Ottoman Empire.

As a result of these victories, British Empire forces captured Jerusalem and established a new strategically strong fortified line. This line ran from well to the north of Jaffa on the maritime plain, across the Judean Hills to Bireh north of Jerusalem, and continued eastwards of the Mount of Olives. With the capture of the road from Beersheba to Jerusalem via Hebron and Bethlehem, together with substantial Ottoman territory south of Jerusalem, the city was secured. On 11th December, General Edmund Allenby entered the Old City on foot through the Jaffa Gate instead of horse or vehicles to show respect for the holy city. He was the first Christian in many centuries to control Jerusalem, a city held holy by three great religions."

The 12th Battalion War Diary for this period no longer exists, so it is impossible to discover where exactly Stanley Lee was mortally wounded. However, we do know that he died of wounds on 24th December 1917, Christmas Eve, and was buried in the British military cemetery in Jerusalem, in grave C.21.

Stanley's mother Elizabeth died on 7th April 1923, aged 50, and was buried in Matlaske churchyard. Robert Lee passed away on 20th November 1944, aged 73.

General Sir Edmund Allenby entering Jerusalem on foot,

December 1917

Stanley Lee's grave in Jerusalem

Stanley Herbert Rouse, 2/2nd Battalion, London Regiment (Royal Fusiliers), C Company, Number G/67256, Died 3rd April 1918 (though some sources say 31st March 1918), Buried at the Chauny Communal Cemetery British Extension, Aisne, France, grave 5.G.11

Stanley Herbert Rouse was born in Little Barningham in the third quarter of 1898. His father was Walter George Rouse, an agricultural labourer, known as George, and his mother was Martha Elizabeth Rouse née Hancock. His family roots were very much in the Barningham and Itteringham areas.

Stanley appears to have had eight brothers and sisters in all. In 1901, the family lived at No 3 Sand Hole in Little Barningham. In 1911, ten members of the family lived in a five-roomed house in the same village. Stanley was still a schoolboy then.

The war memorial in Matlaske church tells us that Stanley was in the 2nd Battalion of the London Regiment. This is not very specific, for the Regiment had 28 battalions numbered 2/1st to 2/28th, plus a 1/2nd, 3/2nd and 4/2nd. However, other sources clearly say that Stanley was in the 2/2nd Battalion (and in fact – an unusual level of detail – in C Company of that battalion).

During the course of the Great War, the London Regiment actually had two 2/2nd Battalions. The first was formed in London in September 1914. This battalion served in Egypt and at Gallipoli. In April 1916 it was sent to France, but in June of that year it was disbanded at Rouen.

Was Stanley a member of the first incarnation of the 2/2nd? This seems unlikely. *Soldiers died in the Great War 1914-19* tells us that Stanley enlisted at Cromer, but not when. It does say that before joining the London Regiment, he was formerly in the 29th Territorial Reserve Battalion with service number 18679. The reserve battalions were not numbered like this until 1st September 1916, so it seems likely that Stanley volunteered when he turned eighteen that September.

We know that from June 1916, the 3/2nd Battalion of the London Regiment was renumbered as the 2/2nd and moved to Ipswich and then to Wiltshire in July before landing at Le Havre on 22nd January 1917. In all probability, Stanley was re-assigned to this Battalion while it was training in Wiltshire.

The big story about Stanley's time in the Army is that his unit was in the thick of the fighting at the time of the so-called Kaiserschlacht, ie, the German Spring Offensive of 1918. This onslaught, in which the German Army in the West was immensely strengthened by troops transferred from the Eastern Front following the Kaiser's peace treaty with Soviet Russia, broke through the British line.

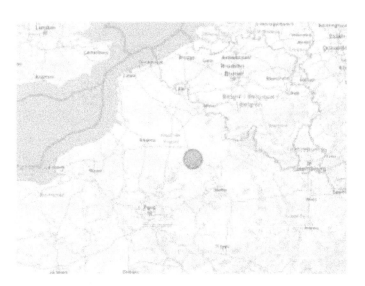

The roundel shows the location of La Fère, where the 2/2nd London Battalion were stationed on the front line at the time of the German Spring Offensive in 1918. This is where Stanley probably received his mortal wounds (© OpenStreetMap)

The success of the German Army in infiltrating the British trenches is described in the table below, which documents how the 2/2nd London Battalion moved around to new defensive positions to try and stem the German advance. The table is based on the 2/2nd Battalion's War Diary. The movements amounted to 15 miles, which is not static trench warfare!

21 March	In the forward zone, opposite La Fère
22 March	Withdrew to Tergnier and defensive positions at Buttes-de-Rouy, then to Viry-Noureuil and Ognes
23 March	At Chauny
24 March	To Abbécourt
25 March	Defence of the bridgehead at Quierzy
26 March	To Besmé
28 March	East of Manicamp, 1.5 miles south of Abbécourt, where the Battalion stayed until 1 April.

The Battalion stayed at Manicamp until 1st April 1918, when it was relieved by a French unit in what was effectively the new Allied front line. It then moved to Blérancourt and Audignicourt nearby before being moved out of the area completely.

What happened to Stanley in these events? We can piece together the sad and rather moving story from the slight evidence we have.

First, we know that he was taken prisoner by the Germans. This is stated in the Register of Soldiers' Effects, which says that he a was prisoner of war at Dercy, a commune just behind the German lines, where he died on 31st March 1918.

There is a query over the correct date of death, as the Commonwealth War Graves Commission has 3rd April 1918. We shall return to that question in a moment, but Dercy makes sense as a place of detention, as it is the next commune to Crécy-sur-Serre, where Stanley was first buried in a German-controlled cemetery.

Second, we know that Stanley was very badly wounded before he died. Evidence provided by the Commonwealth War Graves Commission shows that he had lived long enough to be given pioneering medical treatment for bone fractures. Stanley seems from the Commission's records to have first been buried by the Germans in a military cemetery at Crécy-sur-Serre, near Saint-Quentin. There was a cross on that grave, saying 'Private Stanley Rouse, 2/2 London R. C Coy. 3-4-18'. He was exhumed from here on 13th August 1920. No effects were found on the body, and there was neither uniform nor identity disc. However, both legs and the left arm were in wire splints. These devices sound like the Thomas Splint, which was introduced in 1916 to help reduce deaths from infection following fractures. The extensive use of this splinting suggests that Stanley was badly wounded in a shell explosion. We do not know whether this treatment was administered by British or

German medics. Although it was a British innovation, the German Army presumably developed a similar treatment.

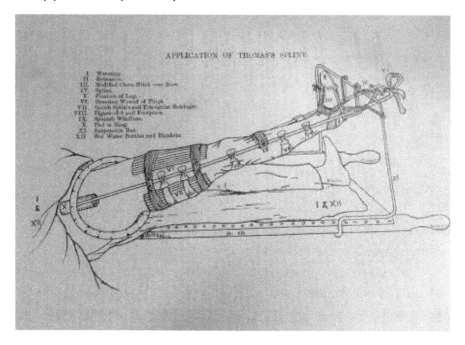

The Thomas Splint

Third, on what day did Stanley die? The evidence I think is that 3rd April is the correct date of death, as this is what the earlier sources said and is also the date finally chosen as correct by the War Graves Commission.

- An exhumation report dated 21st October 1920, following an exhumation on 13th August 1920, states that the cross on the grave said: 'Private Stanley Rouse, 2/2 London R. C Coy. 3-4-18'. This is the document which also mentions the wire splints.
- A graves registration report form dated 29th January 1921 for Crécy-sur-Serre (Group Cemetery Bois de Richmond) states Stanley's date of death as being 3rd April 1918.
- A burial return for the concentration of graves (exhumations and burials) dated February and March 1925

gives the location of the first burial at Crécy (using both French and German grave numbers) and the means of identification (stated to be Cross, GB List and Khaki). This gives the date of death as 31st March 1918

- A graves registration report dated 14th and 21st September 1925 for reburial in Chauny cemetery gives the date of death as 31st March.
- The headstone at Chauny British Military Cemetery gives the date of death as 3rd April 1918.

Fourth, I think it is likely that Stanley was captured by the German Army when his Battalion was resisting the first onslaught of the Kaiserschlacht at La Fère. The artillery bombardment was likely to be more intense there, and La Fère is much closer to Dercy (prison camp) and Crécy-sur-Serre (first burial).

There is no definite explanation for the puzzle over the date of death, but I think it is highly likely that Stanley was mortally wounded in the initial fight against the Kaiserschlacht. The Battalion War Diary sums up the casualties from the 21st to the 28th March as 21 Officers and 650 Other Ranks. Stanley was most probably one of these. The Germans clearly infiltrated some of the British trenches during this fighting, and perhaps Stanley, badly wounded, was captured then. Maybe his Battalion recorded him as missing presumed dead on 31st March. But this is conjecture. The War Graves Commission rightly took the inscription on the cross at his initial place of burial as being correct.

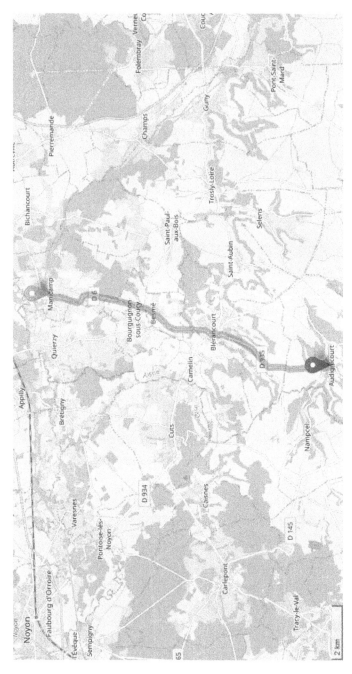

The Battalion's movements from 1st April 1918 (Manicamp)
to 3rd April (Blérancourt and Audignicourt) © Open Street Map

The 22 miles between sites of Stanley's first and final burials (Crécy-sur-Serre and Chauny, respectively) © Open Street Map

By 1918, Stanley's parents lived in Long Road, Colby. On the next page is a form in which his father Walter gave details of Stanley for the Chauny cemetery register.

Stanley's mother, Martha, seems to have been nominated by Stanley as his sole legatee in the event of his being killed, but she herself died in the final quarter of 1918. The Register of Soldiers' Effects shows three attempts by the Army to pay £13 18s 5d to first George, then Martha, and then (after seeing Martha's will) George again in 1918 and 1919. A further payment of £4 followed in December 1919.

CEMETERY REGISTERS.

The whole of this form should be filled up to the RIGHT OF CENTRAL LINE and
returned as early as possible to the address printed on the back. The form requires no postage
stamp and can be folded on the lines marked.

PLEASE WRITE CLEARLY.

CEMETERY _____

Surname ... ... **ROUSE**,

Rank ... ... Pte.

Christian or Forenames (in full) ... Stanley Herbert,

Regimental Number ... ... G/6725C.

Military Honours ... ...

Particulars of Company, Battery
etc., and, in case of Naval Units,
the name of the ship should be
given ... ... Royal Fusiliers (attd. to
Royal Fusiliers, attd.
2nd Bn. London Regt (R. Fus).

Nature of death (if desired and if
particulars are available)...

Date of death ... ... 3rd April, 1918.

Age 19

Give both parents, and native
place of soldier (if desired) Son of Walter George & Martha Rouse
Long Road, Colby, Aylsham Norwich
Norfolk.

Husband of

Wife's address (if desired) ...

Any other particulars in reference
to soldier (if desired) ...

Pla ...

Row ...

Grave ... ...

PLEASE WRITE CLEARLY.

(Signed) Walter George Rouse Relationship Father

Address Long Road, Colby
Nr. Aylsham Norwich

COMPARED FOR

WALTER ERNEST ENGLAND, Number 18598, 9th Battalion, the Norfolk Regiment, Died 18th October 1916, Commemorated on the Thiepval Memorial to the Missing, Pier and Face 1C and 1D

Walter England was born on 15th August 1887 in Cromer.

Walter's father was Henry England, who in 1891 was a domestic servant, living in West Street, Cromer. His mother was Clara (née Lines) and he had two older brothers, Charles and Frederick. Younger siblings, Lillian, Clara and Harry followed some years later.

By 1901 the England family was living at the Dog Kennels in Barningham Winter, where Henry was now employed as a gardener. Walter, aged 13, was an agricultural labourer. The Englands were still living at the same place in 1911, a family of six occupying four rooms.

On 3rd August 1914, the day Germany declared war on France and issued an ultimatum to Belgium to allow its troops free passage, Walter married Ada Celia Money at Holt. The following day, Germany invaded Belgium, and Great Britain declared war.

Ada Money had been born in Little Barningham in 1892, and brought up in Matlaske by her grandparents, Charles and Sarah Ann Money. Charles was a blacksmith whose main business seems to have been making horse shoes. By 1911, Ada was working as a cook at Plumstead Hall.

In November, Walter and Ada had a daughter, Gladys Ada; but after Christmas, Walter, caught up in the patriotic fervour that was sweeping the country, went to Norwich and volunteered to join the Army on 25 January 1915. He was placed in the Norfolk Regiment for the duration of the War.

Extract from Walter England's Attestation Form, bearing his signature

The Army records state that Walter stood 5 feet 7½ inches tall. His chest expansion was from 33 to 35½ inches. He weighed 140 pounds. His physical development was adjudged good, and his pulse rate was 70. He had three childhood vaccination marks. His eyesight was 6/6 for both eyes. He had two large moles below the navel, and had deficient teeth, though the Medical Officer judged that they were not bad enough to cause toothache or poor digestion.

Walter's service record is reasonably complete – many were lost due to enemy action in the Second World War – and from it we can reconstruct the outline of his time in the British Army.

29th January 1915   Posted to the 10th Battalion. This was a reserve battalion, originally formed at Walton-on-the-Naze in October 1914 as a service battalion but placed in reserve on 10th April 1915.

4th October 1915   Posted to the 9th Battalion. This was a service battalion formed at Norwich in September 1914, which had arrived in France on 30th August 1915. I assume Walter crossed the

Channel shortly after his posting but there are no details of his journey in the records.

5th November 1915   Walter was with his battalion in the trenches near Ypres when he received a gunshot wound to the mouth. This is the date given in his service record, which was itself written down on 11th November, but a glance at the Battalion War Diary (an extract is shown below) suggests that he might actually have been wounded on 3rd November, when two Other Ranks are recorded as 'Wounded'.

Extract from the 9th Battalion War Diary – in the trenches near Ypres – November 1915

Walter's Army record seems to show movement between casualty clearing stations, leading to treatment at the military hospital in Étaples, known to the troops as 'Eat apples'.

8th November 1915   Walter was sent to England on the *SS Munich* (spelled 'Munick' in his Army record, perhaps for patriotic reasons; it had originally been a Great Eastern Railway steamship but in 1914 was requisitioned by the Admiralty for use as a hospital ship).

9th November 1915   Walter arrived in the depot. The record does not state where this was.

11th February 1916   Walter was admitted to the War Hospital Croydon for treatment of his gunshot wound to the lower jaw. This seems to have been a fracture of the angle of the jaw on the left side, which in time developed 'bony union' according to the Medical Officer's notes.

24th June 1916   Walter was discharged from the War Hospital.

4th July 1916   Walter was posted to the 10th (Reserve) Battalion

3rd August 1916   Walter embarked Folkestone and disembarked Boulogne

4th August 1916   Arrived at the 17th Infantry Base Depot, and posted to 8th Battalion

Pack mules of the 8th Battalion of the Norfolk Regiment in 1915

2nd September 1916   Walter was posted back to the 9th Battalion of the Norfolks.

18th October 1916   Walter was killed in action. The details of this saddening event will be described below.

It is difficult – because of faded ink - to read the passage in Walter's Army record which notes the date on which Ada, as his next of kin, was notified of his death, but I think it was probably 14th November 1916.

Where Walter was killed

Walter lost his life in a battle that took place in Northern France, not very far from the town of Bapaume, and specifically between the villages of Gueudecourt and Beaulencourt. The site of his loss is somewhere near the D574 road between the two villages, in the bottom left quadrant of the map below. A motorway, the Autoroute du Nord now cuts through the site of the battle.

Another soldier who fought in this same battle was the actor Arnold Ridley, who played Private Godfrey in the BBC TV comedy series, *Dad's Army*. Ridley was in the Somerset Light Infantry, and like Walter attacked the German lines. When he reached the enemy trenches, Ridley, having survived devastating machine gun fire, was knocked down by a blow to the head from a German rifle-butt; then he was bayoneted in the groin and the left hand. The head injury plagued Ridley for the rest of his life, and nearly destroyed his acting career.

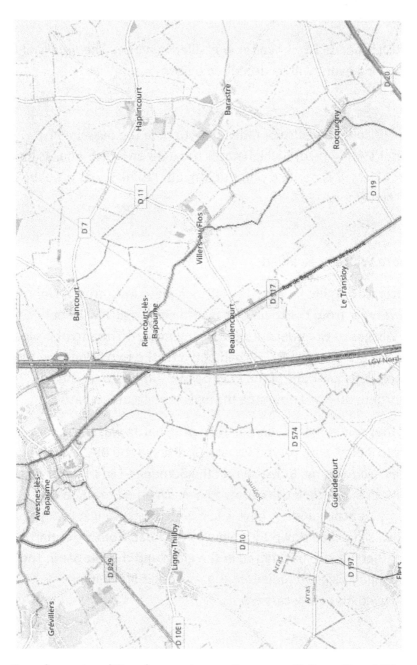

Gueudecourt and Beaulencourt, near Bapaume © Open Street Map

Events on 18th October 1916

The Battle of the Somme has attracted a reputation as one of the deadliest ever fought by the British Army, from the slaughter on the sunny day of 1st July 1916 when it started, to its rain-sodden end in October of the same year, when Walter England lost his precious life.

Walter was killed in the Battle of Le Transloy, which was the final attack by the British Fourth Army in the Battle of the Somme.

The general context of the Battle of Le Transloy is well described by Major General Sir Thomas Marden in his book, *A Short History of the 6th Division*, 1920, pages 25-26:

"After consolidating its ground [in earlier fighting] the Division was relieved by the 20th Division on 30th September, and the long struggle began for the possession of the high ground overlooking the Bapaume-Le Transloy Road. On 7th October the XIV Corps (20th and 56th Divisions) attacked with only partial success, and the 6th Division was brought in again on night 8th /9th October for a general attack on the 12th October. The enemy had dug a series of trenches named by us Rainbow-Cloudy- Misty-Zenith, etc., a portion of which had been captured by us, making a somewhat pronounced salient. All three brigades were in the line, with one battalion in front trenches, the 71st Infantry Brigade (Brig.-Gen. E. Feetham) being in the salient, with the 16th Infantry Brigade on the right and the 18th Infantry Brigade on the left. The objective of the attack of the 12th October was the line of trenches running north from Le Transloy. At 2.5 p.m. the flank brigades attacked, but with only partial success. The failure to make ground, which was general all along the British front, was attributed to want of surprise, as we had bombarded the position for two days, and always attacked in the early afternoon. Further, the ground was very heavy and observation extremely bad. The Germans were fresh troops, and fought well. Perhaps more than anything it was due to the effect of their machine-gun fire. Taught by our creeping barrage that machine-guns in the front line were useless, the enemy had drawn them across the valley towards the road, and caught our advance over the brow of the rise with accurate distant machine-gun fire. Changing the time of zero, the attack was renewed at 5.35 a.m. on the 15th October, the 18th Infantry Brigade on the left (2nd D.L.I, and 11th Essex) attempting to seize those portions of Cloudy and Mild trenches still held by the enemy, while the Sherwood Foresters on their right attacked some gun pits which lay about 200 yards in front of their line. This latter attack succeeded, but with the great loss of Colonel Hobbs, O.C. The Foresters, who died of his wounds. The left attack made a little ground. A final attempt to push forward the line was made on the 18th October by the 9th Norfolks, but was only partially successful. On 20th October the Division (less artillery) was relieved and moved to the First Army, going into Corps Reserve of the I Corps, with Divisional Headquarters at Bethune and the units in the town and surrounding area."

The Wikipedia article on the fighting of 18th October also summarises very well the situation in which Walter made his sacrifice: "On most of the brigade fronts, assembly positions had been marked with white tape and compass bearings taken of the direction to the objectives but at zero hour, the British positions were flooded. The moon was obscured by low clouds, troops slipped and fell in the mud and weapons were clogged, leaving only hand grenades and bayonets with which to fight. On the right the 4th Division attacked with the 11th Brigade to take Frosty, Hazy, Rainy and Dewdrop trenches, while in the French sector the attack began at 11:45 a.m. Groups of the 1st Rifle Brigade reached the gun-pits before Hazy Trench and were forced back, the 1st East Lancs were forced under cover in front of Dewdrop Trench, by the fire of hidden machine-guns. The 1st King's Own of the 12th Brigade and the German defenders mutually attacked and counter-attacked around Spectrum Trench and then the King's Own bombed along Spectrum for 70 yd (64 m) towards Dewdrop Trench. In the 6th Division, the 9th Norfolk attacked Mild and Cloudy trenches but was bombarded before zero hour and moved so slowly through mud that it lost the barrage. The battalion captured the north-west end of Mild Trench and then repulsed a counter-attack as dark fell."

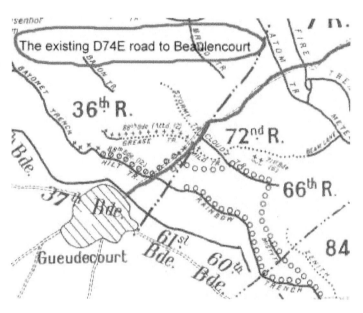

Trench map, with modern annotations in bold – Mild and Cloudy Trenches in the centre

Map showing the Somme battlefield from July to November 1916. Walter England died near the village of Gueudecourt, south of the town of Bapaume, top right quadrant of this map, on 18 October 1916

The 9th Battalion War Diary has this brief overview, day by day, of the fighting in which Walter fell:

16.10

Battalion moved up to line at 4.30 P.M. and took over front held by 18th Infantry Brigade with 1st Leicestershires in support. Relief complete 4.30 a.m. on 16th inst.

17.10

Support line subjected to very heavy bombardment about 5.30 P.M. but suffered few casualties.

18.10

Attack launched at 3.40 A.M., part of Mild Trench being successfully occupied.

Casualties 239 O.R. and the following officers.

Killed

2/Lt Page T.S.

Wounded

2/Lt Beesley R.G.G

2/Lt Clarke J.W.

Capt Rowell, C.G.S.

2/Lt Henshall, H.H.

2/Lt Cowles, W.R.

2/Lt Granestock

Missing

2/Lt Page, J.C.

2/Lt Badcock, H.J.

(18 O.R. joined for duty)

19.10

Communication trenches dug back from Mild Trench. Battalion relieved at 11 p.m. by 1st Worcestershires.

B H L Prior   Lt Col

After the attack, Colonel Prior, the 9th Battalion's commanding officer, wrote a three-page memorandum analysing why the attack had not been a success. He mostly attributes this to the heavy fighting earlier in the Battle of the Somme at the place known as The Quadrilateral, which led to shortages of experienced company commanders and non-commissioned officers, but also says that heavy rain made it impossible for his troops to keep up with the creeping barrage of British artillery fire, leaving them exposed to heavy German counter-fire.

Here is a photograph of the first and last pages of that rather long memorandum, followed by a transcription for ease of reading:

Report on Operations on 18th October

By

Lt. Colonel B.H.L. PRIOR,

Commanding 9th Battalion, Norfolk Regiment.

On receipt of Operation Orders to take over the line held by the 18th Inf. Bde. I met the O/C D.L.I. and West Yorks and arranged for guides to meet the Battalion at 18th Inf. Bde. H.Q. at 5 p.m. Only two guides from the D.L.I. were there and relief was delayed three hours pending the arrival of the West Yorks guides. The guides when they did arrive were most indifferent but the relief was effected with one casualty only, by 2 a.m. My distribution had been A.Coy. right half front line, C.Coy. left half, D.Coy. left flank, bombing posts and sap, B.Company support trenches.

I visited the line at day-break and as the line seemed crowded drew out C.Coy. into RAINBOW TRENCH. I met the G.O.C. in the front line and subsequently returned with him to Bde. H.Q., where the details of the attack were settled subject to his orders.

On my return I got cut written orders for the attack and saw the whole of my Company Commanders and explained my wishes. Orders from the Brigade did not arrive till late which was unfortunate as it precluded my going round the line with my Company Commanders.

During the whole of the afternoon the Battalion was subjected to a heavy bombardment at times growing intense and many casualties were sustained. In addition a heavy rain set in making the ground a quagmire. At midnight I again went round the line and found that the positions allotted were not properly taken up. I was engaged for three hours endeavouring to put things straight. The rain had converted the trenches and "No Man's Land" into a quagmire. Although the men had been instructed to cut steps in the parapet to enable them to get out quickly at zero, the clay was so saturated with water that it was most difficult to get out of the trench.

I went over the top from the front to support lines in which was the second wave and could only make the slowest progress, each shell-hole had become a slimy sticky obstacle. I knew then that it would be impossible for the advance to be carried out under the barrage, i.e., however willing, it was a physical impossibility for the troops to advance at the rate fixed. The G.O.C. had placed a Company of 1st Leicestershires at my disposal for the attack but I decided not to use them for the following reason:-   The attack determined upon could not be carried out on the lines planned in the weather conditions existing. It must either fail totally or partially or succeed because the enemy was suffering equally from the adverse conditions prevailing. It was of course not within my province to postpone the attack, other troops being involved in the assault and I could not communicate with the G.O.C. because I had to go round and personally see to things that would not have been necessary had my Coy. Commanders been more experienced and better trained. I therefore decided not to put the Coy. of Leicestershires into the assault but hold them in hand so that if the assault failed I should have sufficient troops to hold the line against counter attack.

At Zero the assault was launched but in the circumstances described the troops were not immediately under the barrage at the start and could not keep up with it, as a result when half way across, the Bosche had opened an extremely fierce gun and M.G. fire. Two platoons of the right Coy. lost direction and went over to the right, the centre Coy. inclined to much to the left. Despite heavy losses parties of the first line succeeded in entering the Bosche trenches and if it had been possible for the second wave to have moved up promptly, the whole line would I think have been captured and consolidated. The second wave were slow, lost direction and only a few joined up with the first wave the remainder returning to SHINE TRENCH. After the assault had been launched, I returned to Battalion Headquarters but after waiting a long time and receiving no information I went up to SHINE TRENCH to make a personal reconnaissance. On my way I received the first and only message sent from the front during the whole day. This was from 2/Lieut. Cubitt and was to the effect that his platoon had made their objective but was flanked by Bosche on both sides and was short of bombs and ammunition. I at once organised a bomb carrying party. This was taken out by 2/Lieut. Blackwell, who throughout the whole operations shewed extraordinary gallantry and fine leadership; the Bosche were cleared out and junction established with 2/Lieut. Cubitt's platoon. This was in the West end of MILD TRENCH and 2/Lieut. Blackwell at once took over command and organised this trench for defence and establishing a junction with the 2nd Hants Regt. at the Sunken Road.

During the whole day this captured trench was subjected to heavy bombardment and M.G. fire and at nightfall was counter attacked by the Bosche in two waves under a heavy barrage. The assault was checked by two Lewis Guns and by the Garrison throwing out Hand Grenades. Their rifles were choked with mud and the men had nothing dry and clean left to clean them with. Twice during the day this trench and SHINE TRENCH were heavily bombarded by what appeared to be our own Artillery.

I could get no definite information as to what had happened on the Right and Centre but it appeared that though the Boche position had been entered in several places the attack as a whole had failed on this part of the front. Men of the Right, Centre and second wave Companies were scattered promiscuously along SHINE TRENCH and I gave orders for their re-organization and removal to the support and RAINBOW Trenches. This was effectually carried out and the front line re-established as follows:- SHINE TRENCH "A" and "C" Companies 1st Leicestershire Regt., MILD TRENCH and supporting saps "D" Company 9th Norfolk Regt., Support Trench "C" Company 9th Norfolk Regt., RAINBOW TRENCH "A" and "B" Companies 9th Norfolk Regt.

Two platoons of my Right Company undoubtedly got into CLOUDY TRENCH North of the Suffolk Regt. line but I have not been able to find what happened to them.

Another platoon of the Centre Company also reached the Boche line and late in the evening it was reported to me that some of them had been seen in the Boche Trench. I detailed a party under 2nd Lieut. DYE to try and get in touch with this platoon but on leaving the trench the Boche put up such a big machine gun fire that I ordered the platoon to withdraw and ordered 2nd Lieut. Blackwell to send out a strong patrol after dark to ascertain if this party was in fact in MILD TRENCH. 2nd Lieut. BLACKWELL took over this patrol and went upwards of one hundred yards along MILD TRENCH without seeing any signs of this party. He also noted that on this frontage the Bosche had apparently evacuated the trench. The relief of the line by the 1st Worcestershire Regt. was effected by 12.30 a.m.

I should like to bring the following facts to your notice:- I took over the command of this Regiment on the first instant on their coming out of the trenches. The Battalion had lost 20 Officers in the attack on the QUADRILATERAL and in addition to the Adjutant, Q.M., L.G. Officer and Transport Officer had only five Company Officers left.

Of these, three were badly shaken. The Battalion had been converted into two provisional Companies under the command of Major LATHAM, now Commanding the Suffolk Regt. and two days previously Major LEWIS of the Leicestershire Regt. had joined as second in command. The Regiment suffered to the extent of four hundred and seventy casualties at the QUADRILATERAL and had been filled up with drafts, many of whom were little trained.

I had therefore to entirely reform the Unit, find Company Commanders and Officers and make new N.C.O's throughout the unit. I carried this out to the best of my ability. On the 5th October a batch of 9 Officers arrived and subsequently other Officer drafts came in. With one exception they were all Second Lieutenants and I had therefore to pick out three Company Commanders from 2nd Lieutenants. While I have the greatest admiration for the way these Officers endeavoured to carry out their duties I am bound to say that they had not sufficient training or experience to at once assume command of Companies in the field. On taking over the trenches I found that I had to see into matters and carry out work which the Company Commanders, had they had the necessary training, would have relieved me of.

The men behaved extremely well in the most trying circumstances. The majority had not been under shell fire before and were called upon to make an attack after a very heavy bombardment and whilst they were wet and cold and the ground was a perfect morass. The behaviour of "D" Company was exceptionally fine. They were under constant shell fire, machine fire and rifle fire during the whole time they were up but every time I visited them they were cheerful. The Bosche came out three times against them, once the serious counter-attack under barrage already referred to, but each time they repulsed him.

I should like to draw attention to the fact that the drafts now sent out from home do not appear to have adequate instruction in the value of the rifle. I noticed, not only in the case of my own unit, but also in the case of the two Leicester Companies attached to me, that they made no real attempt to shoot the Bosche though there were ample opportunities. On the other hand the Bosche snipers obtained complete mastery and killed a number of our men without any adequate retaliation.

While I deeply regret the failure of the attack on the right and centre, I am certain from the spirit shewn by Officers and men that had weather conditions been favourable they would have been successful. At the same time the failure is partly due to the fact that the Company Commanders, while trying their best, had neither the experience nor the training to adequately organize and lead their Companies in the Field. Moreover they had not had a sufficient opportunity of getting to know their N.C.O's and men.

(Sgd) B.H.L. Prior

Lt. Colonel,

Commanding 9th Battalion Norfolk Regt.

(previous page) The modern road from Gueudecourt to Beaulencourt, which crosses the site of the left ends of first Mild Trench and then Cloudy Trench

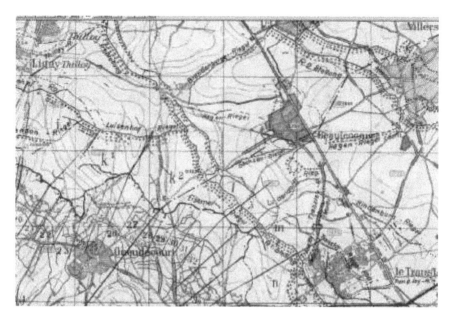

German trench map of the area. This map shows the location of the Luisenhof (top left quadrant), a German position, from which place the photograph below of the battleground today is taken

This is a panorama of the land on which Walter England most likely lost his life. Walter would have been fighting from the right of the picture to the left, probably in the middle distance.

Walter has no known grave, so either his remains were recovered but were not identifiable or they were never recovered.

The Thiepval Memorial to the Missing, Somme, France, designed by Sir Edwin Lutyens, inaugurated by HRH The Prince of Wales in the presence of the President of the French Republic on 1st August 1932. This is where Walter England's sacrifice is commemorated by the nation.

Chapter 6

Nineteenth century

Rectors of Matlaske

This chapter gives more detailed biographies of the nineteenth-century Rectors of Matlaske. The date range is actually longer, extending back into the eighteenth century and forward into the twentieth century. The huge changes that occurred over that period are illustrated by considering the military technologies with which the first and last of these Rectors can be associated – namely, Nelson's HMS *Victory* and the Sopwith Camel fighter aeroplane!

1793-1837   Benjamin Suckling

Born 1767 and died 1837

Perhaps the most notable thing about Benjamin Suckling is that he was a first cousin of Vice-Admiral Lord Horatio Nelson, the victor of Trafalgar. Nelson's mother was his aunt. It is not surprising, in the British euphoria that followed the destruction of the French fleet, and given the grief the whole nation felt at the Admiral's heroic death in battle, that Mr Suckling gave his first son, Maurice, born in 1812, the middle name of Nelson.

Captain Maurice Suckling

It was an earlier Maurice, namely Captain Maurice Suckling (pictured), the uncle of both the Rector of Matlaske and the famous Admiral, who started Horatio Nelson off on his naval career by giving him a place - first as an ordinary seaman, and then as a midshipman - on his vessel, *HMS Raisonnable*, in 1771.

Benjamin Suckling was born in 1767 to William and Elizabeth Suckling, née Browne. His father was Comptroller of Customs, and lived in Kentish Town in Middlesex but also at Banham Haugh, Norfolk. His grandfather, the Reverend Maurice Suckling (pictured, below), was a Prebendary of Westminster. His mother was Elizabeth Browne.

Revd Maurice Suckling DD (1675-1730)

Educated at Tonbridge School, Benjamin matriculated at Trinity College, Cambridge in 1787 and graduated BA in 1791 and MA in 1794. Taking holy orders, he was ordained deacon in 1791, and priested the following year. He served his curacy at Lord Nelson's village, Burnham Thorpe, with his by this time rather ill uncle the Reverend Edmund Nelson, and with his clergyman cousin, Suckling Nelson, the sailor's brother. In 1793 he became Rector of Matlaske and Plumstead and settled down to a long ministry in this quiet and pretty part of Norfolk.

Providence might seem to have marked Benjamin out as a lifelong bachelor, but in 1808 he married twenty-two years old Sarah Spence at Wiveton. He seems to have lived at Edgefield Mount, in Plumstead and sometimes in Holt – presumably in Nelson House, now the offices of Holt Town Council, where an inscription was recently discovered under the lead flashing of the porch, saying "B

W Suckling 1828" – taken to be a reference to Benjamin's son, Benjamin William (1815-1881).

Notable ancestors of Benjamin Suckling include Sir John Suckling, who was Secretary of State to King James I and Comptroller of the Household to King Charles I, and his son, also called Sir John Suckling, the cavalier poet, who wrote very frank romantic poetry but also *An Account of Religion by Reason*, a theologically radical tract. Benjamin's great-great-grandfather Robert Suckling was High Sheriff of Norfolk in 1664. Another ancestor of the Rector, on his mother's side, was his great-great-uncle, Sir Robert Walpole, the first prime minister of Great Britain.

Benjamin Suckling's grave, Plumstead Church

After a long ministry in this quiet part of Norfolk, Benjamin Suckling died in 1837. Given his family's interest in its pedigree, it is pleasing to note that he chose to have a simple tombstone and epitaph in front of the altar of Plumstead church, as befitted his priestly and pastoral role.

Benjamin's widow, Sarah, lived until 1849. In 1841, she was living at Sussex Street, Norwich, of independent means, accompanied by her sons Maurice, also independent, and Benjamin, a chemist, together with her daughter, Mary Parsons, grand-daughter Elizabeth, and Ann Spence, aged 75, described as a nurse, but who I think must in fact have been her mother.

1837-1872   Arthur James Langton

Born 1800 and died 1890

Arthur Langton was the second (surviving) son of Dr Wenman Henry Langton, a clergyman. Indeed, his paternal grandfather and great grandfather had also been clerics, of the Church of Ireland, the former Vicar of Longford and the latter Dean of Clogher.

Dr Wenman Langton was at one time a Chaplain-in-Ordinary to the Prince of Wales, later King George IV, and led divine service at Carlton House.

Arthur Langton was born in Leicester on 8th September 1800, and baptised the following day at St Margaret's church. He matriculated at Wadham College, Oxford, on 17th June 1819, aged 18, and graduated BA in 1823 and MA rather later than normal, in 1837. He seems to have been ordained in 1823 and made curate of Waterden, Norfolk.

Arthur's older brother, Thomas, joined the Royal Navy, saw action in various minor skirmishes, was awarded the Silver Medal of the

National Lifeboat Institution as a Lieutenant in 1830, and rose to the rank of Commander.

In 1826, Arthur married Emily Matilda Gosling, at St Mary Abbots in the parish of Kensington, Middlesex. The marriage bond shows Arthur as being a clergyman, of the parish of Kirton in Lincolnshire. According to family records, the couple were to have eleven children together.

The Old St Mary Abbots, in 1869 shortly before its demolition

In 1835, Arthur became Rector of Beeston Regis, a living which he held only until 1838. From 1837 to 1871, he was the Rector of Matlaske and Plumstead.

In 1841, Arthur was living near the Common in Wickmere, with his wife, seven children and three female servants. The 1851 census has him as the Rector of Matlaske and Plumstead, but living at Couch Green Farm House, Hempstead. Now he has seven children and two servants.

In 1861, Arthur was living at the 'Parsonage / Farm House' in Plumstead, and is recorded explicitly as Arthur Langton MA, Rector of Matlaske and Plumstead. He shared his home with his wife Emily, two daughters (Louisa and Julia) and two servants, the cook Hannah and Mary the housemaid.

When he retired, Arthur Langton showed a great desire to live beside the seaside. The 1871 census has him at 9 Portland Place in Torquay, Devon, with his wife Emily and 29-year old daughter Louisa. He is still the Rector of Matlaske and Plumstead, but only just.

By 1881, Arthur, Emily, Louisa and a servant (Sarah Hughes) were living at 24 Belmont Street in Southport, Lancashire, a rather less benign climate than that of Devonshire. That is perhaps one reason why the family soon moved back to the west country. However, Arthur and Emily also seem to have been following their son, Charles Augustus Langton, around the country. Charles was for many years the Master of Stanmore House Preparatory School in Southport, but in 1883 he retired to Devon, where he later became a Justice of the Peace.

Emily Langton's remaining time with her son Charles was short, for she died in Newton Abbot in 1883. Arthur himself passed away on 30th March 1890. He was then resident at Hillside, Bridge Road, Torre. Probate was granted on 26th April and the retired Rector's estate was valued at £7,335 8s 5d. In today's money, that can be conservatively estimated to be about £728,000.

1872-1883   Arthur James Richards

Born 1843 and died 1928

Arthur James Richards was born on 26th September 1843 at Farlington, Hampshire, where his father, the Reverend Edward Tew Richards (1798-1887) was Rector. Arthur, the fourth son and fifth child, was baptised there on 12th November. Three more brothers for Arthur were to be born later.

In another link between Matlaske and Admiral Nelson, Arthur Richard's mother, Horatia Haslewood, born in 1806, bore the feminine version of the great naval commander's forename; but not through any family connection, as far as I can see, merely as a tribute to the victor of Trafalgar.

The 1851 census found Arthur at Farlington Rectory, with his parents, three sisters, three brothers and six servants (cook, nurse, two housemaids and two scullery maids).

In 1861, Arthur was a visitor at Barton Court, Kintbury, in Berkshire, which appears to have belonged to the Handley family, most of whom were fund holders. The head of the family, who is not actually listed in the census, must have been the senior of the male Handley children, namely, Captain Henry Handley, then aged 26 and an officer in the 2nd Dragoon Guards.

In 1872, banns of marriage were read at Plumstead by the Rector himself for his own wedding; the marriage took place at Chalfont St Giles in Buckinghamshire on 30th April of the same year. Arthur's bride was Margaret Mair Haden (1851-1935), the daughter of John Clarke Haden (1805-1869), the Precentor of Westminster Abbey and Priest-in-ordinary to Queen Victoria.

Barton Court, Kintbury, Berkshire

In 1881, Arthur was at Plumstead, with his son and daughter, and three servants (nurse, cook and house/parlour maid).

In 1891, Arthur was back at Farlington Rectory, but this time as Rector. His father, the previous incumbent, had died in 1887. Arthur's wife Margaret and his son Algernon, his sister-in-law Marion Haden, and two students named Chown, were with him, along with a cook, nurse, parlourmaid and housemaid.

In 1901, Arthur was still in Farlington, but now living in the East Lodge. The Rectory was occupied by a Major Jenkinson of the Royal Field Artillery and his family. With Arthur lived his wife Margaret, their daughter also called Margaret, son Algernon, sister-in-law Marion and two servants, namely, Helen Main Ransome the cook and Minnie Sawyer the parlourmaid.

In 1911, Arthur and Margaret were alone together, but with three servants – cook, parlourmaid and housemaid.

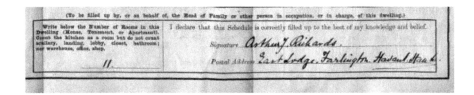

Arthur Richards died on 19 November 1928, at Farlington, aged 85. His estate was valued at £14,248, which is equivalent to about £797,800 today.

Arthur James Richards in later life

Arthur's father, the Revd Edward Tew Richards

Mrs Richards in maturity

Mrs Richards with her oldest child, Harold Arthur David Richards, who later joined the Army and became a Lieutenant-Colonel, saw action overseas with the Army Service Corps, was awarded the Distinguished Service Order and made a Companion of the Order of St Michael & St George

1883-1916   Herbert Wynell-Mayow

Born 1855 and died 1925

Herbert Wynell-Mayow was born at Easton, Wells, Somerset, on 13th June 1855.

Herbert's father, Philip, was a Cambridge graduate and a priest, who served as Vicar of Easton. Philip was originally from Norfolk, his father, also called Philip, being the occupant of Hanworth Hall. Going back several generations, the Wynell-Mayow family seem to have originated in Cornwall.

Herbert's mother, Mary Heath, was the daughter of the Revd Benjamin George Heath of Creeting, Suffolk. Philip Wynell-Mayow and Mary were married at Hanworth on 10th July 1839. They had twelve children, of whom Herbert was the tenth. Not many of the boys made it to mature or late adulthood, though the girls seemed to live longeron average.

In 1871, the family of ten plus a visiting relative (the Vicar's sister) lived in the parish of St Cuthbert out Wells, in the Easton vicarage, along with a cook and two maids. At this time, Herbert was a schoolboy of fifteen.

Herbert was at Sarum College – ie, the Salisbury Theological College – in 1877, was ordained deacon in 1879 and priested in 1881 in Salisbury Cathedral. Between 1879 and 1883, he was Curate of Farley, in Wiltshire, but in 1883 he was appointed to the role he would occupy for well over thirty years, Rector of Plumstead with Matlaske.

Herbert's father died in 1890, and on 6th January 1891 Herbert took a further step in life by marrying Mary Dowling at St Mary's Church, Tyndall Park, Bristol. Herbert must have known Mary since childhood, as they had both been born in Easton, Wells.

18 91. Marriage solemnized at S. Mary's Road in the Parish of S. Mary Tynadalin the County of Gloucester

No.	When Married.	Name and Surname.	Age.	Condition.	Rank or Profession.	Residence at the time of Marriage.	Father's Name and Surname.	Rank or Profession of Father.
234	Jan 9⁶ 1891	Herbert Wynach Mayor	35	Bachelor	Clerk in Holy Orders	Beronstiak Beswick Clifton	Philip Wynach Mayor	Clerk in H.O. Rector
		Mary Dowling	30	Spinster	—	Clifton	Andrew Dowling	Yeoman

Married in the Church of S. Mary according to the Rites and Ceremonies of the Established Church, by or after Banns by me.

	Mayor	
This Marriage was solemnized between us,	Herbert Wynach Mayor	in the Presence of us,	Herbert Beauham
	Mary Dowling		David Beauham Vicar

Herbert and Mary's marriage certificate from 1891

A son, Robert, was born to Herbert and Mary in 1891 but sadly died the following year, aged just eight months. He was buried at Plumstead on 29th June, in a service conducted by the Rector of Gresham.

Another son, Philip John, was born on 13th August 1894. Herbert baptised the boy himself, at Plumstead, on 23rd September.

In 1901, Herbert and Mary were living in Plumstead, with six-year old Philip, and Ellen Lambert, a thirteen-year old housemaid. By 1911, only Herbert and Mary were at home in their eight-roomed house, the Ark.

Herbert's signature on the 1911 Census return

On 31st March 1916, Philip appears to have joined the Royal Flying Corps. As the Masonic records of his initiation into the Suffield Lodge show that he was an engineer after the Great War, it is tempting to suppose that he learned his mechanical skills in the nascent Air Force. Just as the first Rector of Matlaske in this essay had an association with the famous *HMS Victory*, so, perhaps, the last might have had with that notable fighter aircraft, the *Sopwith Camel*.

In 1916, Herbert also completed a move of a few miles, which he seems to have started the previous year, to become Rector of Alby with Thwaite. On 28th May 1925, he died at the Rectory there, and was buried in St Ethelbert's churchyard. Probate was granted in June and the estate valued at £2, 872 9s 5d – which in today's money is about £153,300. That is rather less wealth than some of

Herbert's predecessors had owned, and in its own small way this is probably evidence of the gradual decline in the social status of the clergy over the course of the nineteenth century. On the other hand, the Wynell-Mayow family were able to prove their descent from Plantagenets of the Blood Royal.

Chapter 7

The priest, the shell and the railway

This is rather a sad tale.

The first new Rector of Matlaske to arrive in the twentieth century was Joseph Whiteside, who was born in 1861 in the Lake District and who died there, aged 90, in 1952. He arrived in Plumstead, to be precise about his abode, in the year 1916, following his predecessor's move to Alby.

Joseph was born on 14th May 1861 at Thrimby, which is not too far from Appleby, in the county of Westmorland. His father, Stephen Whiteside (1830-1896), was Vicar of Shap and a landowner who, at his death, was worth about £1.26 million in today's money. Joseph was sent to Durham Grammar School and Trinity College, Oxford, from where he graduated BA in 1884 with third class honours in Literae Humaniores, ie, Greek and Latin.

Marriage followed graduation. In September 1885, Joseph, by now a classics teacher, married Esther Stubbs, the daughter of a hotel keeper, at St Chrysostom's church, Everton, Liverpool.

A son, Cecil Frank Winton Whiteside, was born in Berkshire in April 1887. By 1890, Joseph had been ordained deacon (at Durham Cathedral) and the 1891 census shows him as a curate at Stranton, near Hartlepool, in County Durham, with Esther, Cecil and a servant girl, Martha.

In December 1891, Joseph and his wife had another son, the unusually named Carrol Herbert Marston. This child will figure prominently in our tale of loss.

Joseph was priested in 1892. In the same year, he took up a curacy in Kirkby-Lonsdale. He was made an MA in 1894 and a daughter, Alice Angela, followed in 1895, by which time the family was living in Kirkbride, Cumberland, where Joseph was now Rector.

From 1896 to 1900, Joseph was Vicar of Shap (like his father before him) and chaplain of the local workhouse. In 1900, he also began a year's work as assistant master at Kendal Grammar School.

18_44_. Marriage solemnised at _Whittington Church_ in the _South of Whittington Ditton_ in the County of _Lancaster_

No.	When Married	Name and Surname	Age	Condition	Rank or Profession	Residence at the time of Marriage	Father's Name and Surname	Trade or Profession of Father
427	March Fifteenth	Joseph Whiteside	full	Bachelor	Clerical Teacher	Shop	Westmorland Westland Stephen Whiteside	Clerk in Holy Orders
	18_44_	Esther Stubbs	full	Spinster		Lancaster Road	John Stubbs	Master Draper

Married in the _Church of Whittington_ according to the Rites and Ceremonies of the Established Church, by _Licence_ or after _____ by me, _____ Taylor

This Marriage was solemnized between us { Joseph Whiteside / Esther Smith }   in the Presence of us { Charles W Gibbon / _____ }

Joseph Whiteside's marriage certificate

The 1901 census has Joseph and his family living in the vicarage at Helsington, near Kendal, back in Westmorland, where he is the Perpetual Curate. In 1905 he published a book, *Shap in Bygone Days*. By 1906, local directories show them as living in Brigsteer, part of the same parish. They are still there in 1911, by which time Cecil is a theological student and Carrol a law student.

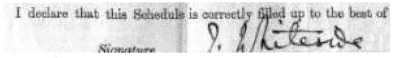

At the age of 55, for reasons we do not know, Joseph decided to move to Norfolk. He took up the living of Matlaske and Plumstead, and presumably settled into a house in Plumstead – though in 1932 he was living at Chestnut Farm, West Beckham.

Joseph and Esther's enjoyment of the gentle Norfolk landscape was soon to be horribly disturbed. In November, 1916, a much-dreaded telegram arrived at the Rectory, announcing the death of their second son, Carrol, in the trenches of the battlefield of the Somme.

Captain Carrol H M Whiteside

18_19_. Marriage solemnized at _the Parish Church_ in the Parish of _Matlaske_ in the County of _Norfolk_

No.	When Married.	Name and Surname.	Age.	Condition.	Rank or Profession.	Residence at the Time of Marriage.	Father's Name and Surname.	Rank or Profession of Father.
74	19 April 1919	Bertie Wiltshire	26	Bachelor	Coachman	Matlaske	William John Wiltshire	Cow-man
		Emma Jane Hannant	22	Spinster	—	Matlaske	James Hannant	Labourer

Married in the _Parish Church_ according to the Rites and Ceremonies of the _Church of England after banns_ by me, _J. Whiteside A.P. Rector_

This Marriage was solemnized between us, { _Bertie Wiltshire_ _Emma Jane Hannant_ } in the Presence of us, { _James Hannant_ _Edith Mary Hannant_ }

The first marriage celebrated in Matlaske church by the Revd Joseph Whiteside, in 1919

Carrol Whiteside was educated at Heversham School, Westmoreland, and then (presumably) read law at Keble College, Oxford, where he graduated BA around 1913. He next became an assistant master at a preparatory school, Stubbington House, Fareham, in Hampshire, which specialised in training boys for commissions in the Royal Navy.

Carrol's surviving Army records are not complete, but it is clear that when the Great War broke out, he joined up relatively early, as he was posthumously awarded the 1915 Star for his early service in France. He joined the 7th Battalion of the Border Regiment, and must have crossed to France with his unit when it landed at Boulogne on 15 July 1915. His initial commission was to the rank of second lieutenant, but the *London Gazette* tells us that he was made a temporary lieutenant in the field and on 4th July 1916 was made a temporary captain. He also served as adjutant of his battalion.

The battalion was assigned to the 71st Division, and helped to hold the front lines in the southern part of the Ypres salient, and took part in various phases of the Battle of the Somme. Skipping over much of the detail, on 29th October 1916 the battalion moved to a camp near Trônes Wood, which had been captured in the fighting on the Somme in July. By now, it was just mud.

The next day, the battalion moved up to a position called GERMAN DUMP and relieved the Rifle Brigade. The trenches – NEEDLE, WINDMILL and MAIL - were in a poor condition and wet, and offered no shelter for the men.

On Tuesday 31st October, the weather was bad. The Germans intermittently shelled NEEDLE and MAIL trenches. Officers went up to liaise with the HQ of the 10th Sherwood Foresters and the 50th Brigade to the right, and made arrangements to relieve the Foresters the next day. Nine men were injured by an enemy bomb which was struck while cleaning up NEEDLE trench. Lt Col W J Woodcock was injured by shrapnel, and Carrol Whiteside was seriously wounded by shell fire which killed three Other Ranks outright.

On 1st November, the battalion relieved the 10th Sherwood Foresters in the front line, and Captain Whiteside died of his wounds.

Carrol was buried at Grove Town military cemetery, at Méaulte, in the Somme area. His father chose 'God bless thee always, brave soul, beloved boy, until we meet again' as an inscription.

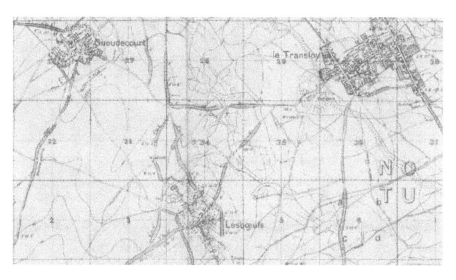

The area where Captain Carrol Whiteside was fatally injured. The battalion moved first to a position in square 33 (middle row), and then probably to the trenches in square 34. This position is near to Gueudecourt and Le Transloy, where other sons of Matlaske perished

On 4th February 1922, Joseph applied to the War Office for his dead son's medals.

The extent of Joseph's grief for and pride in his son is indicated by the memorial works done in his name at Plumstead church, which included the altar, reredos, litany desk and screen, as well as the tablet shown in the photograph below.

Memorial in Plumstead Church

Sadly, the territorial ambitions of other nations in the 20th century were to take a further toll of the Rector of Matlaske and Plumstead.

Joseph's older son was Cecil Frank Winton Whiteside, who had been born at Winkfield in Berkshire in April 1887. He was educated at Selwyn College, Cambridge, graduating BA in 1909 and MA in 1913. In 1917, Cecil married Dorothy Angela von Tobel at Clitheroe in Lancashire. She was the daughter of a Swiss merchant who had settled in Great Britain. In 1919, Dorothy gave birth to a girl, Norma Angela. A son, Carrol Eugene, followed in 1920. Both children had Von Tobel as a middle name on their birth certificates, but did not use it.

Like his father Joseph, Cecil Whiteside became a priest. He was ordained deacon in Lincoln Cathedral in 1912, and priested the following year. However, he seems to have found it very difficult to get a living. He served as a curate in many locations - in Lincolnshire, Yorkshire, Norfolk, Nottinghamshire and Derbyshire - before finally moving to Holbeach St John in Lincolnshire.

While in Yorkshire, Cecil was also Reader of Waddington Hospital, near Skipton.

When war broke out in 1939, Cecil was living in the rural parts of Grimsby. His son, Carrol Eugene, evidently joined the British Army for he became a Gunner in the Royal Artillery, number 1770691, and was posted to the Far East. He served in 7 Coast Regiment. Some documents say 9 Coast Regiment, but in practice the two units were barely distinguishable, according to veterans. Both were central to the defence of Singapore. 7 Coast Regiment manned two 6-inch guns at Beting Kusha Battery, and three 15-inch guns at Johore Battery. However, the Japanese conquest of British Malaya and the imminent threat of losing Singapore led to the destruction of the coastal batteries on 12th February 1942. The artillerymen marched to the Indian Recreation Ground, where they were formed into an infantry battalion and used as support troops; but the British garrison as a whole surrendered on 15th February.

Along with many other men, Carrol Whiteside became a prisoner of war.

The extraordinary sufferings of military prisoners in the Far East make a man living comfortably today shudder in horror. Carrol found himself working on the Thailand-Burma Railway. He died on 30th May 1943, aged 23, and was buried in some local spot near the track. His remains were later exhumed by the Commonwealth

War Graves Commission and reburied in the Kanchanaburi War Cemetery in Thailand, in grave 2.F.7.

Bridge over the River Kwai by Leo Rawlings, a prisoner of war who was involved in the line's construction. The sketch has been dated to 1943

The fact that Carrol's body was relocated to this cemetery indicates that he worked on the southern part of the railway, between Ban Pong and Nikki. This segment includes some notorious locations, such as the Bridge on the River Kwai, and the cutting at Hellfire Pass. Carrol died in May 1943, and the first wooden bridge over the Kwai was completed in February at that year. A ferro-concrete bridge was completed in June, shortly after Carrol's death.

Of course, we cannot be sure that Carrol Whiteside worked on this particular section of the railway. We do know that when he died, he was first buried in the Kanburi paper mill cemetery, grave 12, and was exhumed and reburied in the Kanchanaburi cemetery on 29th January 1946.

Carrol's grave in Thailand

The inscription chosen by the family was 'In loving memory of our dearest son Carrol. RIP. Father, mother and Angela'. I have not been able to determine exactly when these words were chosen. That question is significant, because Cecil Whiteside did not survive his son for long. The grieving father himself died, at Kings Lynn, on 25th January 1944, aged 56. Was the inscription chosen by his widow?

Map of the Thailand-Burma Railway

But what of Carrol's grandfather, Joseph Whiteside, who had been Rector of Matlaske until 1942, according to the board displayed in St Peter's church? He had lost a son, Carrol, in the Great War. His daughter, Alice Angela, appears to have died in Norfolk in 1931. At the time of the 1939 Register, he was staying in a hotel or lodging house at 122 Highgate, Kendal, Westmorland, but without his wife Esther. And then his grandson Carrol dies in 1943 in the Second World War, followed not long after by this Carrol's father (Joseph's son), Cecil. Then Joseph's wife Esther dies in Hereford on 9 February 1945.

I sense that the old man drew to the close of his own life troubled by gloom, but hoping for reunion in light perpetual.

Joseph himself died on 4th April 1952 at Corner Cottage, Shap.

Chapter 8

RAF Matlaske

This chapter is mostly based on Janine Harrington's booklet, *RAF Matlaske 1940 – 1945, A Brief History,* published in 2014; excerpts are reproduced with her kind permission.

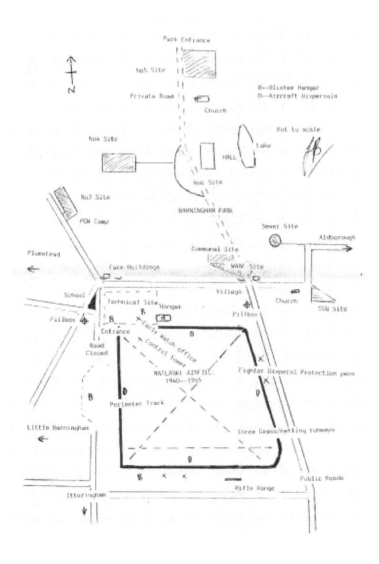

Reminiscences

"Matlaske I found so different – lovely quiet rural countryside. We interpreted the move as a rest for the pilots, many of whom had served long days during the Battle of Britain based at Hornchurch, Essex.

"There were no runways at Matlaske. It was just a large grass field with some blister hangars and a small Watch Tower, but very few buildings. We were billeted in a stately home, Barningham Hall. It was a handsome building, but with all furnishings removed the rooms were bare except for Service beds and 'biscuits' (servicemen's expression for the narrow mattresses on which they slept). Some of us were in a small room in the top storey.

"The Cookhouse, the Airmen's Mess and NAAFI were in outbuildings and stables in the Hall courtyard. When our work on the aircraft was complete, we were allowed time off on some afternoons and we spent many lazy hours by the lake in the Park near the Hall and walking in the Gardens and fields close by.

"Being a 'Townie', I decided to send some country fare home to my folks. Calling at what was the local village Post Office cum everything-else shop, the only one in the area; hesitantly I asked if there were any eggs to spare. To my amazement, the young shop assistant in a rich friendly broad Norfolk accent (which I love!) asked: 'How many you want, two score?' I never expected there would be so many eggs available during such an austere time. I purchased the lot, packed them very carefully in a strong tin and sent them home. Alas, on arrival, my parents found the tin had been bayoneted by our Censor or someone! It had done the eggs no good at all."

Frank Webster, 'Instrument basher', 222 Squadron (at Matlaske 6 May 1941 – 30 June 1941)

"The pilots were sitting around their coke stove in readiness. But one day, a tractor driver got his coat caught in the wheel. He was thrown off and injured while the tractor continued on ... in and through the pilots' hut, wrecking the stove and setting fire to the building. At least one pilot was injured.

"I started keeping a diary while at Matlaske with notes about the Hall and village. But it was taken off me during a kit search at Waterloo Station. They said it contained names useful to the enemy!"

Arthur Sadler, Electrician, 137 Squadron (at Matlaske Dec 1941 – Aug 1942)

Squadrons stationed at Matlaske

SQUADRON	AIRCRAFT	DATES	FROM / TO
72	Spitfire 1	Oct-Nov 1940	From Coltishall
222	Spitfire 2	May-July 1941	From Coltishall
601 (City of London)	Hurricane 2	July-Aug 1941	From Manston
19	Spitfire 2	Aug-Dec 1041	To Ludham
5 Air Sea Rescue	Walrus	Oct 1941	From Coltishall
278 ASR	Walrus	Oct 1941	Formed from 5 Flight, Aug 42 to Coltishall
137	Whirlwind	Dec 1941-Aug 1942	To Snailwell
56	Typhoon1	Aug 1942-July 1943	To Manston
245	Typhoon1	May 1943	From Gravesend
266	Typhoon1	Aug 42	From Duxford

609	Typhoon1	Jul-Aug 1943	From Manston
1498 Target Tow	Lysander, Master, Henley, Martinet	Apr-Jun 1943	Coltishall
56 Group USAAF	Thunderbolt	Mar-May 1943	Air firing practice
611	Spitfire9	June 1943	Short rest
19	Spitfire5b	June 1943	Bomber escort
195	Typhoon1	Jul-Aug 1943	Coltishall
Closed for reconstruction work, August 1943. Placed under Care & Maintenance control. Then occupied by 3rd Aviation Engineer Battalion, US Army, March to April 1944			
3	Tempest5	Sep 1944	Short rest
56	Tempest5	Sep 1944	Short rest
486 RNZAF	Tempest5	Sep 1944	Short rest
19	Mustang3	Sep-Oct 1944	Bomber escort
65	Mustang3	Sep-Oct 1944	Bomber escort
122	Mustang3	Sep-Oct 1944	Bomber escort
229	Spitfire9	Oct-Nov 1944	To Swannington
453 RAAF	Spitfire9	Oct-Nov 1944	
602	Spitfire9	16 Oct-Nov 1944	
451 RAAF	Spitfire16	Feb-Apr 1945	
Army Co-op Unit	Auster AOP	Jul-Oct 1945	Airfield closed

At its peak, there were 2,500 personnel based at RAF Matlaske.

Royal Visit

King George VI and Queen Elizabeth visited RAF Matlaske on 28th January 1943 and met pilots from 56 Squadron.

Some Incidents

12th Feb 1942 – Maximum effort by 137 Squadron to escort five destroyers. Aircraft were intercepted by twenty Me 109s which were escorting enemy battleships *Scharnhorst* and *Gneisenau*. Four RAF Whirlwinds were shot down.

4th May 1942 – P/O Red Wright was killed when his aircraft broke up mid-air in during a combat exercise

27th May 1942 – Brennan and Le Gelle on patrol, sighted and shot down a Ju 88 20 miles off Cromer. Brennan continued patrol and failed to return. [Note: Ft Sgt John Robert Brennan was killed the same day. Buried at Bergen General Cemetery, Netherlands.]

29th May 1942 – P/O Jowett – engine fire on return from patrol, bailed out to land by parachute on doorstep of the Officers' Mess, which he had left an hour earlier. The aircraft went on to crash at Sheringham.

19th August 1942 – Bryan and Roberts scrambled, sighted a Do 215 off Happisburgh, which they shot down in flames.

8th December 1942 – 'Rhubarb' (ie, low level Seek & Strike attacks) to Knocke area gun posts (in Belgium), a hangar, goods train and barges were hit. P/O Wright bailed out of R7846 which got into a spin. Wright known as 'Lobster' because of his ruddy complexion, boasted after his third accident he had broken more Typhoons than anyone.

9th January 1943 – F/O Rouse killed when his Typhoon was shot down by flak near Kijkduin.

20th January 1943 – Mid-air collision between two Typhoons. Both crashed near Blickling, one pilot killed.

15th March 1943 – Sgt Nettleton hit by flak in the Ijmuden area, attempted forced landing on beach where he hit a mine, exploded; he was killed.

18th March 1943 – USAAF 303 Group B-17 Flying Fortress heavy bomber – forced landing at Matlaske after being shot up on ops with three crew injured.

17th April 1943 – Engine failure off Cromer, crashed into sea. F/O Cluderay found dead in dinghy.

6th August 1943 – Typhoon DN361 crash landed at Plumstead.

11th October 1944 – Mustang FB127 crashed on approach to land at Matlaske.

1st April 1945 – Spitfire SM249 crashed while taking off.

Possibly a photograph of men of 137 Squadron (motto: *Do right, fear naught*) at RAF Matlaske, sometime between December 1941 and August 1942

The aircraft in the photograph above are Westland Whirlwinds, twin-engine heavy fighters. Residents living near Matlaske usually saw 12 to 16 take off each day. "Those who flew the Whirlwind either loved or hated it. It was not an easy aircraft to fly and its accident rate was high. Many pilots remarked: *'If only it could have had Merlin engines!'"*

Inspired by Janine's research, I have looked at some of the operational logbooks from RAF Matlaske myself. There is one episode that I should like to share, as it brings out a range of things about the RAF aircrew: their good judgement, their sense of humour, pride in their skill, and dedication to duty; but also, their humanity. It is an entry dated 3rd April 1943 in the Operations Record Book for the No 56 (Punjab) Squadron, stationed at Matlaske:

> "In the evening Operations called for six A/C to go on a special mission to attack a suspicious looking trawler, which had been reported by some Spits to be lying about 35 miles off Petten on the Dutch coast, with a peculiar looking mast. Operations seemed to think it was a wireless ship so ordered the attack. F/Lt. Piltingsrud and Sgt. Magee were to be top cover to the other four, but the former's engine began to behave strangely so they turned back and landed at 1845, having taken off with the others at 1810. The other four, F/Lt. Dredge, F/O. Cluderay, F/O. "Lobster" Wright and Sgt. Birks, found the trawler just about where it should have been, but could see nothing on it that looked suspicious, except that Sgt. Birks saw a thing which looked like some sort of tube running up one side of the mast. Anyway, they attacked, "Lobster" drawing first blood, and also the first blood in his career, this being his first effort at the enemy. The whole show was too easy, as there was no opposition of any sort. Nobody was seen on board but the vessel got under way very rapidly as soon as "Lobster" fired. The four Typhoons then formed a sort of circle and

kept going round firing in turn, F/Lt. Dredge getting in three bursts and the others five each. It was set on fire well and truly, and as they flew away after their 18 attacks, large flames were seen coming from the cabin and deck house aft, and a trail of smoke some 300 yards long. The only hitch about the whole show is that the pilots think they have pranged some inoffensive Dutchman out on his lawful occasions, which rather detracts from the satisfaction of having done a good job well and truly."

As the father-in-law of a Dutchman, I find this very poignant.

One other fact is worth mentioning. As we saw above, on 18th March 1943, an American Flying Fortress, a huge bomber, had to make an emergency landing at RAF Matlaske. Len Bartram in his booklet on Matlaske airfield says that the Fortress had taken part in a raid on Bremen, was badly damaged and had wounded men on board. David W J Brown, in his excellent book *Matlaske: The Village of my Youth*, records that the Fortress overshot the airfield and crashed into the hedge on the side of the road halfway between Matlaske and Squalham. Jeremy Norman tells me that the hedge in question is still missing. It was at the summit of Wickmere Road, at the spot where (if you are travelling away from Matlaske) there is a small gap in the hedge to your left giving access to the footpath to Pear Tree Farm, and a gaping gap to your right.

Chapter 9

A Matlaske man at Omaha Beach

It was Napoleon Bonaparte who founded the Legion of Honour, France's highest decoration for civil or military merit, in 1802. How many French novels involve characters who are desperate to sport the coveted ribbon of the Legion in their button-holes? It is remarkable, therefore, to discover that a modest man of Matlaske, Donny March, is actually a Chevalier, that is, a Knight, of this distinguished order; and that he was given this signal honour for his part in what most people think was a uniquely American operation, namely, the deadly D-Day landings at Omaha Beach in Normandy, France, on 6th June 1944.

Donny's route to the dangerous seas off Omaha Beach began modestly enough in the quiet village of Plumstead, just a mile or so from Matlaske. Eager to serve in the war effort, he had joined the Royal Observer Corps and had a post in this neighbouring village, where he learned to identify different kinds of aeroplane, and distinguish friendly machines from enemy ones. He was just 17 years old when, in May 1944, he was informed of a call for men to serve as aircraft spotters at sea. The details were still top secret, but in fact the job was to serve on the merchant ships that were then being lined up to take part in the invasion of France.

Donny went home and talked the challenge over with his father, the village blacksmith (and undertaker), Clifford March, who agreed that he should go if he wanted to. When Donny went back on duty, he discussed the matter again with a friend, Alec McBain-Smith, who was an Observer in Cromer; and the two young men decided to volunteer together.

Things began to move rapidly. Donny and many other men from the Observer Corps were enrolled as Petty Officers in the Royal Navy, and given uniforms bearing the shoulder flash SEABORNE as well as the Royal Navy brassard. After just two weeks of intense training, and a medical examination, Donny was sent to Southampton, where he was paired with a Welsh lad of his own age. They were then taken to the Greenock naval base of the Home Fleet, on the south bank of the River Clyde, which was under constant German air attack, where they were assigned to the SS *Jim Bridger*, a Liberty class American merchant marine ship named after a 19th century frontiersman and pioneer.

Donny and his mate were given a kindly welcome by the African-American crew of the *Jim Bridger*. The ship was capable of carrying about 480 men and their associated vehicles and supplies. Once the new Petty Officers were aboard, the ship weighed anchor and steamed off to Southampton. This was the first time Donny had ever been to sea. After a couple of days or so, they docked in Hampshire. The final destination was still secret, but not long after steaming off again they could see that they were part of a huge operation. Hundreds of other ships were converging on the same destination. The sky was full of enemy aircraft, the sea was full of mines and there was a risk of being attacked by E-Boats.

The *Jim Bridger* dropped its anchor a mile or so off the French coast, its crew and passengers now realising that they were about to play a part in the long-awaited D-Day. In front of the ship was Omaha Beach. The beach was full of obstacles, the defences were strong; engineers struggled to clear obstacles; landings could not be made where planned; under deadly Nazi fire, many men were killed as they disembarked from landing craft.

Donny and his comrade had a platform on either side of the ship, the Welshman to port and Donny to starboard; the platforms were equipped with a cannon and a copious supply of ammunition. But more important than shooting the cannon, for Donny and his mate, was to give a good steer to American anti-aircraft gunners by correctly identifying German and Allied planes. This they did by the simple expedient of looking through binoculars, and then giving their assessment by a direct radio link to the ship's captain. Otherwise, says Donny, the Americans would have fired at anything!

Enemy aircraft were everywhere. Many ships had been hit. Casualties floated in the sea. The *Jim Bridger* was under constant fire, but Donny and his mate kept to their task for three or four days despite getting little sleep. The ship's captain was then able to discharge his cargo of troops and equipment with relatively few casualties and little damage.

As soon as it became clear that the footholds on the beach would hold, the ship steamed off to Falmouth to pick up more soldiers and their gear.

By the time the ship returned to Omaha Beach, US troops ashore had made substantial progress, and the *Jim Bridger*, no longer needed to ferry reinforcements, was ordered back to Southampton.

His D-Day mission successfully completed, Donny volunteered for the Army. He first joined the Royal Norfolk Regiment and then the 2nd Battalion of the Suffolk Regiment. Whilst in the Army, he served in India. He left the Army early in 1947, and returned to Norfolk to take up an apprenticeship as a wheelwright, eventually becoming a carpenter.

Donny married his wife Ruth in 1959.

Donny was awarded the Legion of Honour for his part in the Liberation of France by the French Consul, M. Jean-Claude Lafontaine, at a ceremony on 23rd January 2016.

Donny in the Army. Second row (from front), third from right

Donny with his Legion of Honour decoration

Chapter 10

Matlaske Hall

Where was it?

At the eastern end of the village, roughly where the modern barn is at Hall Farm. If you walk along the track behind the farm, you can still see a garden wall with the imprint of a now demolished hot house on it.

When was it built?

The Hall is usually described as Georgian, which could be anything from 1714 to 1830.

It certainly appears on the 1839 Tithe Map. The Gunton family, who owned it, seem to have come to Matlaske from Wickmere by at least 1735 - when Robert and Rachel Gunton's eldest son, Whitaker Robert Gunton was christened at Matlaske church.

(Incidentally, 'Whitaker' is a recurring Christian name in the Gunton family, and seems to be a tribute to Richard Whitaker (1687–1730), a Matlaske resident who was High Sheriff of Norfolk in 1725. Was he related to the Gunton family, perhaps by marriage? I have been unable to prove this.)

White's Directory of 1854 describes Matlaske Hall as 'a handsome modern mansion, delightfully situated'. The 1885 Ordnance Survey and the 1839 Tithe Map look to me as if they are showing the same building.

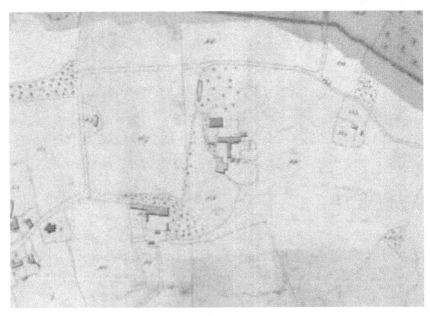

Tithe Map of 1839

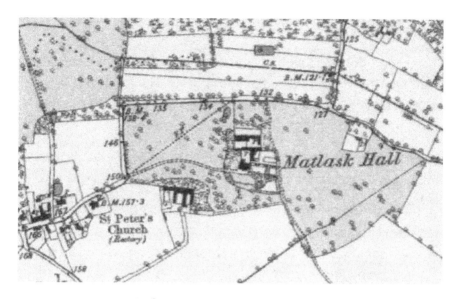

Ordnance Survey Map of 1866

What was it like?

149

The Hall

The **ground floor** had a dining room, a ball room, a drawing room with two bay windows and, communicating with the drawing room, a panelled library. There was also a gun room, lavatory and side and back entrances.

This floor had, in addition, a Housekeeper's Room, Servants' Hall, Kitchen, Scullery, Dairy, two Larders, a Butler's Pantry and a WC.

On the **first floor** – approached by two staircases – were seven bedrooms, four dressing rooms (each also capable of taking a bed), plus two servants' bedrooms, a bathroom and WC, various cupboards and another WC.

On the **second floor**, there was another bathroom and four attics.

The Estate

When it was put up for sale in 1951, the whole estate had 366 acres.

The outbuildings of the Hall itself were:

- Sun dial and miniature rock garden
- Tennis and croquet lawns
- Two kitchen gardens: in one was a lean-to vinery; in the other, a greenhouse, small vinery and potting shed
- Orchard
- Back courtyard including garage, stalls, harness room, coach house, hay loft, kennels, wood shed and a water pump

Kenneth Argent was the tenant of the Hall between about 1951 and 1954, where he ran an older people's home. He had moved this business from Aldeburgh, Suffolk, bringing with him his four children. Vera Fairweather assisted him, as did her sister Thelma, who married Vic Wells from Itteringham and settled in Matlaske and neighbouring villages. Kenneth Argent's son, Michael, who now lives in Australia, has made the following sketch plan, from memory, of the ground floor as it was at that time. Credit is due to Ben Wood for turning the sketch into an engineering drawing.

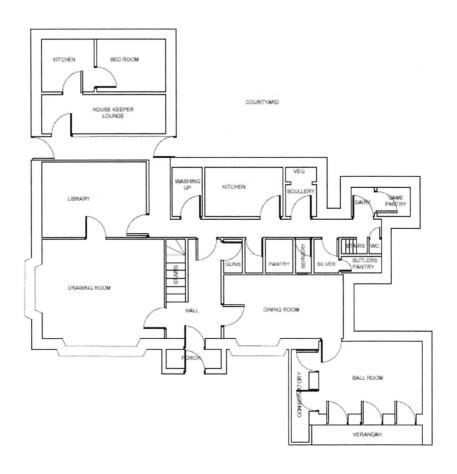

Matlaske Hall – Ground Floor Plan, circa 1952

By Direction of George Lee, Esq.

NORFOLK

Aylsham 7 miles, Holt 6 miles, Norwich 20 miles, in a first-class agricultural, sporting and social district

FREEHOLD   IN LOTS

The Important Residential and Agricultural Property

known as

The Matlaske Hall Estate

of about

366 ACRES

and including Georgian Residence in Timbered Parks, with extensive farm premises and 8 cottages and nearly 350 acres.

VACANT POSSESSION

of all but the cottages.

THE FREEHOLD HEAVILY TIMBERED
MATLASKE WOOD of 13 ACRES

with

VACANT POSSESSION

NINE COTTAGES and CARPENTER'S SHOP
IN MATLASKE VILLAGE

WHICH MESSRS.

IRELANDS

IN CONJUNCTION WITH MESSRS.

R. C. KNIGHT & SONS

will offer for sale by auction in nine lots (unless previously sold privately)

At THE ROYAL HOTEL, NORWICH,
On SATURDAY, 30th JUNE, 1951,
At 2.45 p.m.

Particulars and Conditions of Sale from the Solicitors —Messrs. Hansell, Hales, Bridgwater and Preston, 72, The Close, Norwich (Tel. Norwich 20079), or from the Joint Auctioneers —Messrs. Irelands, Bank Plain, Norwich (Tel. Norwich 20745), and Messrs. R. C. Knight & Sons, 1, Upper King Street, Norwich (Tel. Norwich 24284/80), 130, Mount Street, London W.4 (Mayfair 0224/4) and Branches.

Who lived there?

Censuses and yearbooks give us some information about the Hall's owners and occupants:

1841 – Dennis Gunton (1770-1842) and his wife Louisa (1782-1844) plus two adult children, Dennis and George, and Frances, Dennis junior's wife live there; with four servants.

1851 – Frances Gunton (1804-1869), now a widow, is living there alone, with six servants.

1861 – Frances Gunton owns the place but is away on a journey; she still has six servants.

1871 – the Reverend John Gunton (1806-1890) is now the owner, but not resident. He is also the Rector of Marsham and lives there. George Lee (1825-1892), a farmer of 300 acres, employing 14 men, 3 women and 5 boys, may be resident in the Hall with two relatives and a housekeeper, but the census return is not clear.

1881 – John Gunton is still the owner, but the occupant is Herbert Cook (1852-1923), a farmer of 350 acres, employing 9 men and 4 boys, along with his wife Edith, daughter and three servants.

1890 – John Gunton dies, and ownership of the Hall passes to his younger brother, George Gunton (1813-1896), a farmer, of White Hart Street, Aylsham.

1891 – a tenant, George Osborne Springfield (1843-1893), occupies the Hall, along with his wife Evaleen, three children, a governess and six servants. Mr Springfield is a retired lieutenant of the 5th Dragoon Guards, who in 1875 had divorced his aristocratic first wife. He dies at the Hall.

1896 – George Gunton dies, and ownership of the Hall passes to the Revd George Montgomery Norris MA (1828-1914), Rector of South Cove, Suffolk, who according to the 1912 Kelly's Directory is lord of the manor and chief landowner. Mr Norris's paternal grandmother was Rose Gunton (1769-1805), so he is George Gunton's first cousin, once removed.

1896 – Kelly's Directory for this year shows that Neil McLean (1836-1923), a prosperous merchant and shipowner, is now the tenant. His wife is Elizabeth. Registers of electors also show Mr McLean to be in Matlaske between 1897 and 1899.

1901 – another retired Army officer, Major John Sloman (1830-1901) now lives at the Hall with his wife Lydia, their granddaughter, a governess and six servants. Major and Mrs Sloman were married in India in 1859. After leaving the Army, the Major became a farmer, maltster and brewer.

1902 – Robert William McConnel is born at Matlaske Hall on 13th September to Dr Henry Wilson McConnel (1859-1938), a retired Army surgeon and his wife, Mary Louisa. Young Robert suffered from an oesophageal stricture and was not strong. His father did not think he would be able to follow him into the practice of medicine. However, Robert proved capable of obtaining the BA in natural sciences at Clare College, Cambridge, and then of qualifying as a doctor at King's College Hospital in London. He graduated MB BCh in 1931 and began a notable career in private practice. He died in 1964.

1904 – Kelly's Directory shows Henry Wilson McConnel as the tenant still. Dr McConnel is the son of a wealthy Manchester cotton spinner, and a Cambridge graduate. He is also Major John Sloman's son-in-law. The McConnel's daughter, Cicely, had actually been staying at Matlaske Hall with her Sloman grandparents at the time of the 1901 census.

1911 – Henry McConnel remains the Matlaske Hall tenant but is away at census time. His gardener, Daniel Boulter (1873-1942), with his wife Lina, six children and a niece, is looking after the house.

1930 – The McConnels still have tenancy at Matlaske Hall, as well as a home in Sussex.

1933 – Kelly's Directory shows that local farmer George Lee (1885-1974) is now lord of the manor and chief landowner.

1941 – The Hall (or perhaps just part of its grounds?) was commissioned as a military hospital, according to British Geological Survey records of a well bored there in August 1941. This is probably connected with the RAF Sick Quarters that stood where the houses on The Green are now.

1951 – The Hall was sold by George Lee to Rex Carter (1916-2001). Kenneth Frederick Argent (1903-1972) and his family arrived as tenants and ran an older people's home in the Hall for several years.

1954 – The Argents left the Hall.

What was it like to live or work there?

Michael Argent lived at Matlaske Hall as a teenager, and has happy memories of learning about farming and gamekeeping in the area. After serving in the Merchant Navy, he emigrated to Australia and, building on his Norfolk experience, set up probably the first pheasant farm in Tasmania.

Donny and Ruth March say the Hall was lovely. Donny has memories of George Lee's daughters, Doreen and Kathleen, having grand parties in the ballroom.

Derek England worked at the Hall as an assistant gardener. He describes the gardens as beautiful. He remembers the Argent family living at the Hall, with Vera Fairweather (who later married Kenneth Argent) hanging her washing out to dry in the heated greenhouse on rainy days!

When was the Hall demolished?

When the Argent family moved to Southrepps, the landowner Rex Carter decided to demolish Matlaske Hall. This would have been around in the latter years of the 1950s.

John Neill bought the farmland and still owns it.

A Note on Sources

Chapter 1

In modern usage, 'Matlaske' refers to the village and 'Matlask' to the civil parish as defined under the Local Government Acts. I prefer to use the former spelling, though some books and websites use the latter to refer to the village or parish historically.

The civil parish of Matlask currently includes the historic parishes of Matlaske, Barningham Winter and Barningham Norwood. All three are of great interest, but my focus so far has been on the village of Matlaske and, to some extent, Barningham Winter.

Dr Ann Williams, Professor G H Martin (editors), 2003, *Domesday Book: A Complete Translation*, Penguin Classics, a paperback, is based on the Alecto Historical Editions of 1992. I have found that this provides a good overview.

The Open Domesday website by Anna Powell-Smith is an excellent resource that enables you to read the original text, if you can handle the Latin and the calligraphy (it can be rather a struggle): see https://opendomesday.org/place/TG1534/matlask/. I have one note of caution, namely, that I think the summary economic statistics given on this website must include the other places mentioned in the same section, not just Matlaske.

On historic buildings and archaeology, the Norfolk Heritage Explorer is very useful. A search such as http://www.heritage.norfolk.gov.uk/search-results?Parish=MATLASK will produce everything of note in the civil parish of Matlask.

Chapter 2

The Wikipedia articles on Barningham Hall and Edward Paston are good places to start. Note, however, that the Edward Paston who built the current Barningham Hall does not seem to have been a knight, despite several sources saying that he was.

Information about the most prominent members of the Wynter family comes from the articles on the website http://www.historyofparliamentonline.org/research/members. This site gives material on several members of the Paston family too, though not Edward, the builder of Barningham Hall, who seems to have carefully avoided public office – probably because of his Catholic sympathies if not allegiance. I found some good clues about Edward Paston in R W Ketton-Cremer's book, *Norfolk in the Civil War*, 1985 edition with an Introduction by Robert Ashton.

Using Cambridge University search engines, I have drawn on a couple of academic papers relating to Edward Paston, namely:

Brett, Philip (1964). "Edward Paston (1550–1630): A Norfolk Gentleman and his Musical Collection". *Transactions of the Cambridge Bibliographical Society*, Cambridge Bibliographical Society. 4 (1): 51–69.

Taylor, Philip (2012). "Memorializing Mary Tudor: William Byrd and Edward Paston's 'Crowned with flowers and lilies'" *Music & Letters*, May 2012, Vol. 93, No. 2, pp. 170-190.

Information about Margaret Paston, whose epitaph was written by the poet Dryden, I have mostly found through research on the Ancestry website.

Chapter 3

This chapter is based largely on information from the Norfolk Heritage Explorer website. I have also consulted Nikolaus Pevsner,

The Buildings of England: North-East Norfolk and Norwich, Penguin, 1962, who does not always agree with the county archaeologists and historic buildings surveyors.

The leaflet on *St Peter's Church, Matlaske* produced by H Holbeach and W J Goode in 1989, revised by D C Wooff in 2005, has been invaluable. I found some extra information about the Norwich bell foundry at http://www.reptonchurch.uk/Bells.htm#bcq.

Simon Knott's website http://norfolkchurches.co.uk/mainpage.htm offers a very readable commentary on the church's architectural and historical merits.

The website https://aroyalheraldry.weebly.com/ is a good source of information on what we usually call coats of arms.

The list of Rectors comes from the church itself. To supplement this, I have drawn on Blomefield's 18th century history of Norfolk, available online at https://www.british-history.ac.uk/topographical-hist-norfolk/vol8/pp136-137, and the Cambridge Alumni records for mentions of Matlask or Matlaske (available on Ancestry).

It is always interesting to compare historical money values with present day worth. I like to use the website www.measuringworth.com.

However, this website gives you an embarrassment of riches: a different result for a commodity, for income or wealth, or for a project; and then within each of these categories, different answers depending on whether you're interested in capital or labour costs or share of overall gross domestic product. For instance, Mrs Gunton's £300 in 1850 could be worth in 2020 as little as £32,320 (real price of a commodity) or as much as £1,220,000 (economic cost of a project). Take your pick!

Chapter 4

The Norfolk Heritage explorer website
www.heritage.norfolk.gov.uk is the key source here, along with
Blomefield's researches available at https://www.british-history.ac.uk/topographical-hist-norfolk/vol8/pp97-101.
Information on the Rectors has been drawn from Cambridge
Alumni records via the Ancestry website. Simon Knott's essay on
Barningham Winter on his Norfolk Churches site is particularly
illuminating.

Chapter 5

The War Memorial in Matlaske Church is the starting point. I have
used Ancestry as the main resource for reconstructing the stories
of these remarkable young men who gave their lives for their
country. Open Street Map is a great resource under open licence
for producing modern maps to illustrate distances; copyright of the
base mapping remains with Open Street Map and contributors.

Other resources that shed light on what actually happened include:
entries for the soldiers on the Commonwealth War Graves
Commission website www.cwgc.org; battalion war diaries and
other military records from Ancestry and/or the National Archives;
Wikipedia, which is replete with excellent articles on units,
formations, campaigns and battles; the National Library of
Scotland, which freely makes Great War trench maps available
online; the Global Find a Grave Index; military history websites
such as www.longlongtrail.co.uk, which is excellent for tracing the
history of units and formations; and the analysis and discussion,
backed by evidence, on websites such as www.greatwarforum.org.

Chapter 6

The starting point was the Rectors Board in Matlaske Church. The rest of the contents of this chapter was almost completely reconstructed from family or local history data made available via the Ancestry website.

Chapter 7

Again, Ancestry has played a key role in providing genealogical data for this chapter. Military questions have been settled using the same kind of resources as in Chapter 5. The 'Every One Remembered' website https://www.everyoneremembered.org/ yielded a photograph of the Captain Whiteside who died in the Great War. The photograph of his memorial is courtesy of War Memorials Online https://www.warmemorialsonline.org.uk/; the picture was taken by Adrian S Pye in 2015, to whom due acknowledgment is made. The Global Find a Grave Index (accessed via Ancestry) yielded the image of the grave marker for the younger Carrol Whiteside.

Chapter 8

This chapter is heavily indebted to the work of Janine Harrington, who is the Secretary of the RAF 100 Group Association, and the author of the booklet *RAF Matlaske 1940-1945 A Brief History*. In addition, I am grateful to Mr Tom Nightingale for his advice on operational records kept by the National Archives, and to the National Archives for permission to use these. I have also consulted the book on Matlaske Airfield by Len Bartram, a copy of which was kindly given to me by Jim Shepherd.

Chapter 9

The main source for this chapter is the document
https://www.rocatwentytwelve.org/uploads/1/2/9/1/12917554/donald_march_d_day_medal.pdf, which can now only be accessed
by finding a cached version in a Google search for 'Donald March
legion of honour'. Other details are available in a newspaper article
from July 2016, a photograph of which is in my possession.
Photographs of Donny March were kindly made available by the
Shepherd family. Information about the SS *Jim Bridger* and the
class of Liberty ships in general has been gleaned from web
searches of the name, which, eg, yields a photocopy of the Lloyds
Register entry (not used for this chapter); on the use of the Liberty
ships, the site http://www.usmm.org/normandyships.html was
helpful.

Chapter 10

The Norfolk Record Office has been invaluable in finding
documentary evidence as to what the Hall was like. I am grateful to
Mr Michael Argent of Rutherglen, Victoria, Australia, for his
personal recollections of living there, and to Mr B J Wood MEng
GMICE who kindly drew up the floor plan from Mr Argent's sketch.
The Norfolk Record Office has given kind permission to reproduce
the tithe map, catalogue reference DN/TA 496, and the Norfolk
Heritage Centre has done the same for the Ordnance Survey First
Edition.

Details about the occupants of the Hall have largely been
reconstructed using directories, census returns, birth, marriage and
death records – all accessed via Ancestry or, in this particular case,
Find My Past, which sometimes gives a better overview of parish
register data for the Gunton family. I have also used online text
from the *British Medical Journal* accessed via Cambridge University
search engines.